Phonemic Awareness Knowledge to Practice

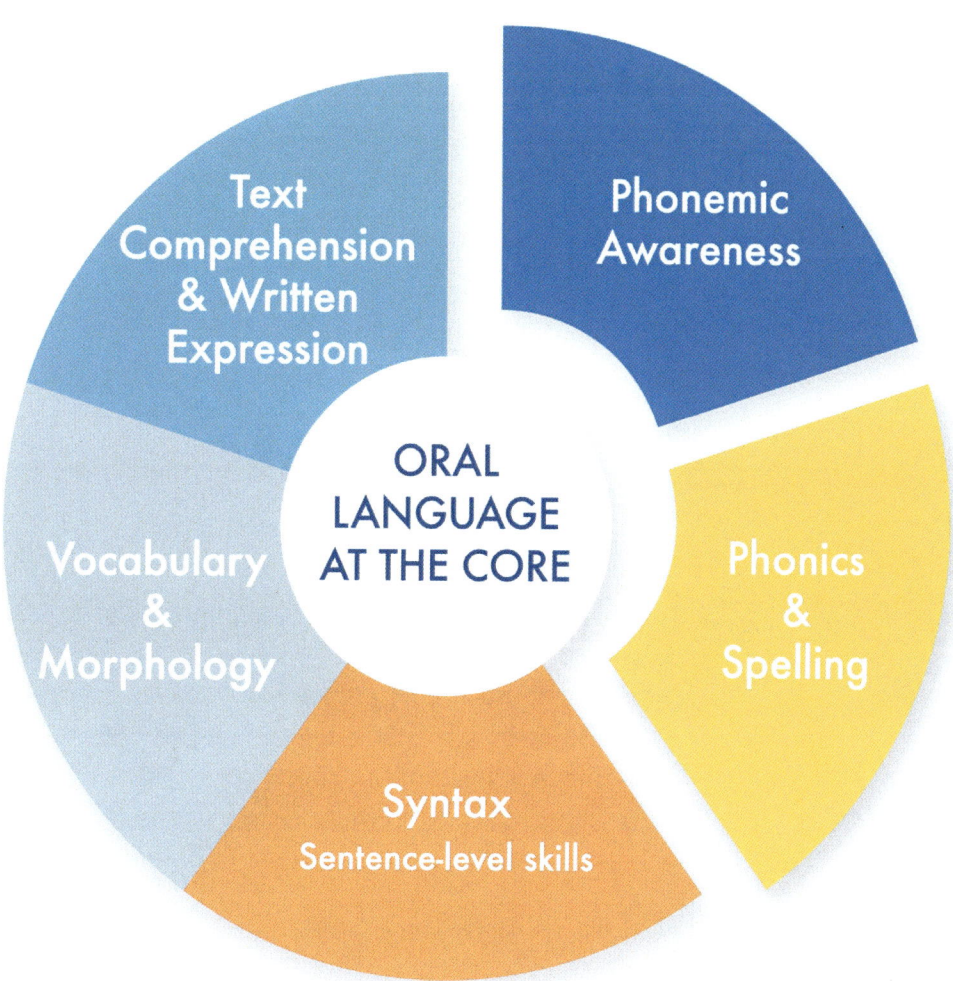

Margie Bussman Gillis &
Nancy Chapel Eberhardt

Copyright © 2018 by Margie Bussmann Gillis and Nancy Chapel Eberhardt

Direct communication to:
Literacy How
www.literacyhow.com

All rights reserved. No portion of this work may be used or reproduced in any manner whatsoever without written permission, except in the case of brief quotations embodied in articles and reviews.

Cover by Liang Design

Other titles in the Literacy How Professional Learning Series:
Syntax: Knowledge to Practice
Vocabulary: Knowledge to Practice
Reading Comprehension: Knowledge to Practice
Available at www.amazon.com

The **Literacy How Professional Learning Series** is dedicated to:

The educational researchers whose work informs our understanding;
The Literacy How Mentors who empower teachers
by translating evidence-based knowledge into classroom practice;
The teachers who tirelessly strive to ensure that every child learns to read;
And the students who are at the heart of all that we do.

Table of Contents

Introduction to the **Literacy How** Professional Learning Series — 1

Phonemic Awareness

Relevant Research in Phonemic Awareness — 5

Knowledge for Effective Instruction — 7

Activities for Instruction and Informal Assessment — 16
    Isolation — 18
    Onset-Rime Awareness — 22
    Segmentation — 25
    Blending — 31

Text Selection Skill Analyses — 33

Phonics

Relevant Research in Phonics — 40

Knowledge for Effective Instruction — 43

Activities for Instruction and Informal Assessment — 59
    Concepts of Print — 62
    Phoneme-Grapheme Acquisition — 64

Reading and Spelling Words . . . 72
Syllable Pattern Identification . . . 82
Phonetically Irregular Words . . . 103
Automatic Word Recognition . . . 107

Text Selection Skill Analyses . . . 112

Appendix . . . 125

 # Introduction to the Literacy How Professional Learning Series

Linking What We Know to What We Do

Literacy How is a professional development organization that has drawn on decades of research to create a current and comprehensive model of how children learn to read. The **Literacy How Professional Learning Series** translates that model into a set of reference and instructional tools for teachers and educators dedicated to developing children's literacy skills. This series links what we know about *how* students acquire literacy skills to evidence-based instructional practices that help them achieve those skills. While the series emphasizes Pre-K-3 conceptual and skill development, teachers of older emerging or struggling readers will also find these reference tools useful in order to understand their students' errors and target interventions based on those errors and their stage of reading development.

The Literacy How Reading Model

The purpose of the Literacy How reading model is to provide a framework for conveying all the elements of literacy required for a child to become a reader, a writer, and a speaker. The Literacy How Reading Wheel below graphically represents those elements. The model builds on the work of Louisa Moats (1999) and the findings of the National Reading Panel (2000). Importantly, it features a core emphasis on oral language in recognition that a young child's oral language skills provide the foundation for all aspects of literacy development. In this regard, the Literacy How reading model goes beyond the National Panel recommendations and includes spelling, syntax, and written expression as significant elements of literacy education.

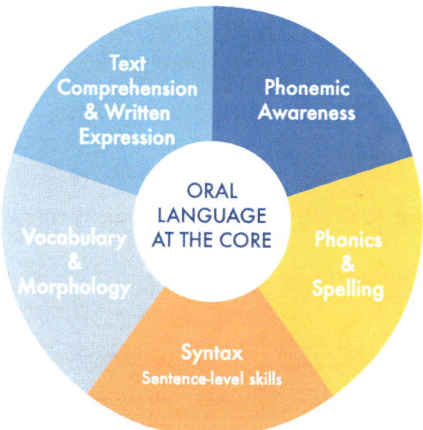

You may notice that fluency, one of the recommendations of the NRP report, is missing from the Literacy How Reading Wheel. That is because the Literacy How model views fluency as essential to all aspects of literacy development. Fluent (i.e., automatic) performances in both discrete and complex literacy tasks are the mark of proficient readers and writers.

Stages of Reading Development

The Literacy How Reading Wheel represents the content of reading instruction but does not delineate the specific elements that should be taught at various developmental levels. We decided it was important to orient the content on typically developing children. For this, we turned to Chall's stages of reading development (Chall, 1983). Stages 0-2 provide a map of students' progression on the road to skilled reading. Key research findings for each stage assist in determining, evaluating, and developing instruction.

The following table displays the three stages of reading development that serve as an organizational framework for the research, activities, and text-based lessons in the Literacy How Professional Learning Series. As with any aspect of child development, progress through the stages can be varied and somewhat serpentine rather than uniform and linear. Regardless of the pace and path, the stages can guide the instructional process. (See Activities for Instruction and Informal Assessment pages 16 and 59 for examples of stage-specific instructional guidance.)

Chall's Stages of Reading Development

	Stage 0	Stage 1	Stage 2
Name	Pre/early reading	Alphabetic	Consolidation
Description	Pre-reading/pretend reading stage: Children learn to recognize and write the letters of the alphabet. The acquisition of phonological awareness is a major development.	Initial reading and decoding stage: Children learn that speech sounds map on to letters to make words and that these words can be read by sounding out each letter or letter's associated sound.	Confirmation and automaticity: Children consolidate their reading skills –decoding, sight word recognition, and comprehension of words and text – and read with increasing fluency.
Oral language layer	Oral language, both receptive and expressive, is the foundation for phonological awareness, as well as background information and vocabulary.	Syntactic awareness and syntactic knowledge contribute to reading. By grade 1, most children have sufficient knowledge of syntax for reading. Most also have a sufficiently large listening and speaking vocabulary. (Chall, p. 62)	The language of most children is sufficient for their reading.
Approximate Grade (age)	Pre-K (3-5)	K-2 (5-7)	2-3 (7-9)
Focus	Alphabetic Principle Oral Language	Decoding Encoding	Automaticity Prosody
Reading component(s)	Listening Comprehension, Phonemic Awareness, Invented Writing		Reading Comp Written Expression
		Basic Phonics	Advanced Phonics
	Vocabulary and syntax throughout		
Text type focus that students read	Predictable	Decodable/hybrid	Familiar text, literature, informational text

Effective Instructional Practices

All aspects of this series are shaped by the use of effective, evidence-based instructional practices. Researchers have identified effective practices to teach literacy concepts and skills, among which are the following: (See "Features of effective instructional practices" pages 13 – 14 and pages 52 – 53 for further explanation of these features.)

1. Explicit instruction
2. Emphasis on making abstract concepts concrete
3. Emphasis on automaticity
4. Development of metacognitive strategies to facilitate transfer of knowledge and skills
5. Stress on cumulative, systematic, and sequential presentation of content and skills
6. Use of data to guide instruction

Types of Text

Just as the content of reading instruction depends on the age/stage of the child, so too does the type of text used for instruction. Early childhood teachers use predictable texts because they are based on oral language patterns and structures – that is, they are characterized by repeated words and phrases that children can easily remember. Another kind of text, code-emphasis, provides students who understand that sounds map onto letters with an opportunity to practice lower-level decoding skills and a small number of sight words. Finally, teachers use authentic text (both narrative and nonfiction) to help more advanced readers develop fluency with self-confirmation of accuracy and ease of understanding.

Text Selection Skill Analyses

The instructional process involves both explicit content and skill instruction, as well as opportunities to apply those skills in text. This requires teachers to choose the text, as well as to analyze how to use it effectively to address the needs of their students. This analytic process involves identifying possible skills within the domain suited to a particular text, and then tailoring skill-oriented activities based on the text. Through this process, any text selection provides an opportunity for teachers to reinforce a wide range of reading skills. (See the Text Selection Skill Analyses section pages 35 and 112 for illustrations of this process.)

Now What?

The Literacy How Professional Learning Series is organized for the busy educator who may be trying to find specific information, as well as for the professional seeking deeper understanding of literacy instruction and learning. You can decide which component of the Literacy How Reading Wheel matches your current purpose/interest. In this case, you have selected **Phonemic Awareness and Phonics: Knowledge to Practice** as your area of interest. This resource combines the two domains—Phonemic Awareness and Phonics—most essential to the development of word recognition (i.e., decoding) skills. You will find the information about each domain divided into Relevant Research, Knowledge for Effective Instruction, Activities for Instruction and Informal Assessment, Text Analyses, and an Appendix. You may wish only to delve into research or you may have a greater need for the activities. It's up to you!

RELEVANT RESEARCH in Phonemic Awareness

What is it?

Phonemic awareness is an awareness of and the ability to manipulate the individual sounds (phonemes) in spoken words. It is a subset of **phonological awareness**, which pertains to an understanding of sound patterns in a language, including word and syllable awareness. Together phonological and phoneme awareness provide a foundational ability essential to acquire and master the alphabetic principle in order to learn to read and spell.

Awareness of the phonological structure of language follows a developmental progression or sequence (See the section "The developmental progression of phonological and phonemic awareness" page 10). For example, children are better able to gain control over larger units of sound (i.e., words, syllables, rimes) before smaller units (i.e., phonemes). Instruction should follow a sequence from larger units to smaller units (Yopp & Yopp, 2000). Therefore, if teaching phonological and phonemic awareness, begin with skills such as identifying the number of words in a sentence, progress to the number of syllables in words, and finally to the smallest units, namely the number of phonemes in words.

Research has provided extensive evidence of the importance of phonemic awareness from a developmental perspective, as well as in terms of specific populations—ELLs, dyslexics, and older struggling readers. Let's take a look at what we know from research in relation to each stage.

	Developmental Sequence		
	Stage 0 (Grades Pre – K)	**Stage 1** (Grades K – 2)	**Stage 2** (Grades 2 – 3)
Focus of literacy development	Pre-alphabetic principle; letter naming	Alphabetic principle Decoding and encoding	Orthographic and morphologic patterns
What do we know from research?	• Sensitivity to larger phonological units – that is, words, syllables, and rhymes – occurs earlier and more naturally than phoneme awareness (Fowler, 1991). Children who are able to recognize rhymes and alliteration easily are often skilled at segmenting and blending individual speech sounds in words. However,	• Phonemic awareness constitutes a necessary underlying skill for mapping alphabetic symbols to spoken words and can be developed through instruction (Ehri, 2004). In fact, teaching phoneme awareness reduces the incidence of reading problems (Shankweiler & Fowler, 2001).	

	Developmental Sequence	
	phonological sensitivity does not necessarily predict later reading success (Bowey, 2000). • "To progress with reading, children must develop the insight that alphabet letters represent abstract speech segments (phonemes) and must be able to compare the likeness and difference of similar sounding words" (Shankweiler, 1989). • Unless children understand that words have sound segments at the phoneme level, they cannot take advantage of the alphabetic script (Liberman, Shankweiler, Liberman, 1989).	• Phoneme awareness is one of the strongest predictors of reading success (Blachman, 1989; Adams, 1990). • Since phonemes are "elusive" because of their very nature (Adams, 1998), instructional approaches that are the most phonemically explicit have the greatest impact (Torgesen, 2002). • While phonological and phonemic awareness lessons and activities are done orally, activities are enhanced when they include concrete representations of sounds in order to make phoneme manipulations – segmenting and blending – more overt (Ball & Blachman, 1991). • Linking phoneme awareness with letter instruction facilitates transfer to reading and spelling (Ehri, 2004). • Teachers must be able to produce phonemes accurately, as well as manipulate these phonemes, in order to teach phoneme awareness effectively (Spear-Swerling & Brucker, 2004).	

English Learners

- Research demonstrates that phoneme awareness assessments predict students' success in learning to read. This has been demonstrated with English speaking students as well as students who speak other languages (Adams, et.al. 1998).

Students with dyslexia/reading disabilities

- The length of time required for a student to reach benchmark goals in phonemic awareness is a strong predictor of risk for later reading problems (Byrne et al, 2000).
- Problems with phonemic awareness are a hallmark of reading disability and are reflected in genetic patterns and patterns of brain activity (Shankweiler & Fowler, 2004).
- Although phonological awareness loses its power to predict reading success as students go through the grades, "it continues to be a strong predictor of reading outcomes for those on the bottom end of the reading continuum who have not adequately developed their phonological awareness skills" (Kilpatrick, 2015).

 **KNOWLEDGE for Effective Instruction**

Defining the "ph" terms

With so many words in literacy beginning with the letters "ph," it is easy to get confused about their meanings. As we begin to discuss phonemic awareness instruction, there are three terms that are particularly important to distinguish—phonological awareness, phonemic awareness, and phonics. These are highlighted in the following table. Phonological awareness is an umbrella term which should not be used synonymously with phonemic awareness. The distinction between these terms has important implications in terms of instruction.

Term	Definition	Examples
Phonological Awareness	Ability to identify and manipulate oral language at the level of word, rhyme or syllable	March to identify each word in a sentence Clap to identify each syllable in a word Categorize words beginning with the same sound Recognize if word pairs rhyme.
Phonemic Awareness	Ability to focus on and manipulate individual sounds (phonemes) in spoken words	Move a token to segment the sounds in **hat**. / h / / ă / / t / Blend these sounds / h / / ă / / t / = **hat**
Phonics	Ability to link spoken sounds to the letter or letter combinations that represent them	/ h / is represented by h / ch / is represented by ch or tch / ā / is represented by ai, ay, a_e, eigh

It is also important not to confuse the difference between the phonemes (sounds) we hear in words with the graphemes (letter symbols) we use to represent them. Phonemic awareness does **not** involve letters. For this reason, when considering the words **hat** and **thatch**, the answer to "How many phonemes in each of these words?" is the same (3), despite the fact that the number of letters used to represent the sounds ranges from three (**hat**) to six (**thatch**).

Word	Phonemes	Letters	Graphemes
hat	/h/ /ă/ /t/	h – a – t	h – a – t
hatch	/h/ /ă/ /ch/	h – a – t – c – h	h – a – tch
thatch	/th/ /ă/ /ch/	t – h – a – t – c – h	th – a – tch

The role of phonics instruction is to teach the letter or letter combinations (graphemes) that represent each sound. It is the relationship between phonemes and graphemes that is a one-to-one ratio. Phonemic awareness provides the essential foundation for children to learn the sound-to-spelling correspondences.

What are we listening for?

When we talk about phonemic awareness, we are talking about the sounds (phonemes) that make up our language. In English, most agree that there are 44 speech sounds organized into two categories—consonants and vowels.

The sounds are categorized according to how they are produced. Consonant sounds restrict airflow during their production. Our speech organs - lips, teeth, or tongue – close off the flow of air. The following chart displays the 25 consonant sounds according to the position of the mouth, which indicates how air is restricted, and the type of consonant sound.

English Consonant Chart

Type of Consonant Sound	Bilabial (lips)	Labiodental (lips/teeth)	Dental (tongue between teeth)	Alveolar (tongue behind teeth)	Palatal (roof of mouth)	Velar (back of mouth)	Glottal (throat)
Stops	/p/ /b/			/t/ /d/		/k/ /g/	
Fricatives		/f/ /v/	/th/ /th/	/s/ /z/	/sh/ /zh/		/h/[1]
Affricatives					/ch/ /j/		
Nasals	/m/			/n/		/ng/	
Lateral				/l/			
Semivowels	/ʰw/ /w/[2]			/r/	/y/		

[1] Classed as a fricative on the basis of acoustic effect. It is like a vowel without voice.
[2] /ʰw/ and /w/ are velar as well as bilabial, as the back of the tongue is raised as it is for /u/.
Adapted with permission from Bolinger, D. 1975. *Aspects of Language* (2nd ed.). Harcourt Brace Jovanovich, p. 41.

*Some systems for counting the speech sounds yield 44 speech sounds.

In contrast, vowel sounds do not restrict the flow of air during their production. They are referred to as open sounds. Vowels are the language sounds that form the nucleus of a syllable. A vowel sound—with or without consonants—forms whole or parts of words. For example, a single vowel sound can be a word such as "I" or "a." A single vowel can also be a syllable in a multi-syllable word, such as the i in item. The number of syllables in a word is equal to the number of vowel sounds (e.g., one syllable in tree; two syllables in meatball; three syllables in volcano).

Vowel sounds are produced by subtle changes in the position and height of the tongue. The following table maps out the vowel sounds. Most vowel sounds are represented by multiple graphemes represented by the list of words below each of the vowel sounds in the table (e.g., long **o** has five grapheme representations: **o**, **o_e**, **oa**, **ow**, and **oe**). For the purposes of phonemic awareness, however, the emphasis is on the sounds only. (See pages 40 – 58 for details about the transition from phonemic awareness to phonics.)

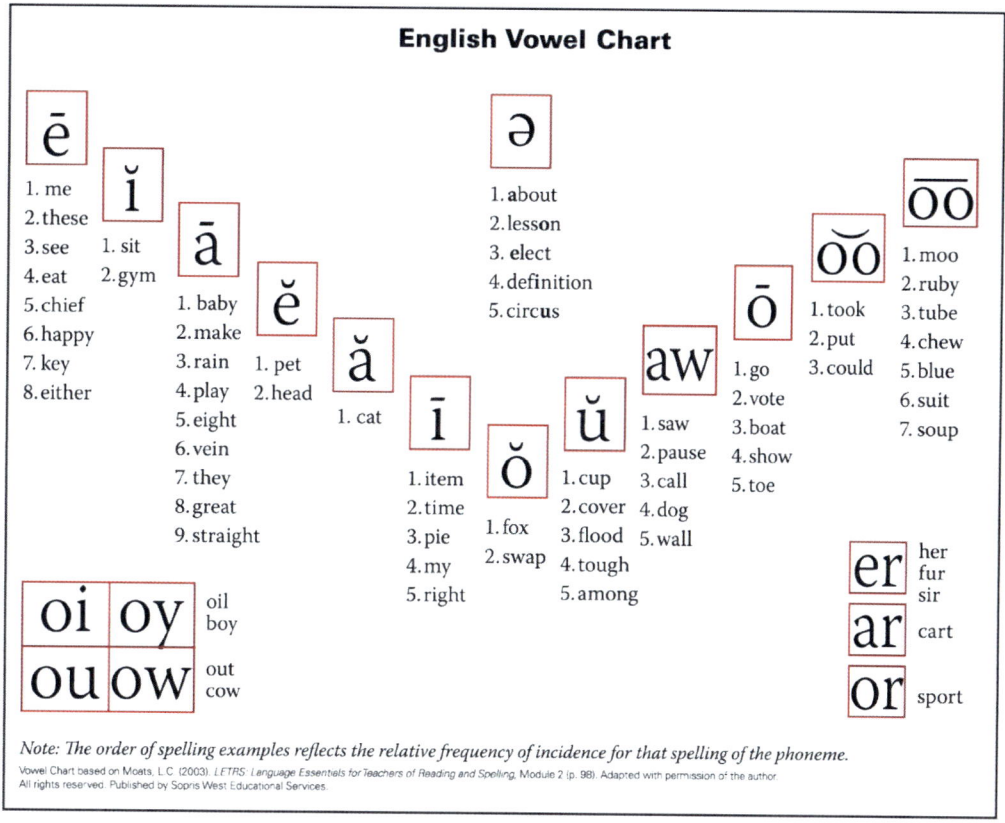

For instructional guidance, see the **Mirror Mouth** activity on page 21.

As teachers, it is important to be knowledgeable about the speech sounds in English, as well as the sounds in their students' first languages. In the case of English learners whose first language is other than English, a contrastive analysis showing differences between the sounds of English and those of other languages is helpful for differentiating instruction. This type of analysis provides insight into which speech sounds in English are not in the student's first language providing valuable information for instructional planning. For example, Spanish does not have the / ĭ / sound in its phonological system. As a result, this sound may be difficult for the student to recognize and/or produce.

Even for students who speak English as their first language, they may speak a dialect and therefore may have difficulty articulating specific sounds. For example, a child from Boston may not pronounce the /ar / sound in **cart** (see English vowel chart on page 9) or a child from Texas may not hear the difference between the / ĕ / in **pen** and the / ĭ / in **pin** due to local dialects. As with English learners, extra attention to the manner and placement of the articulation of sounds as well as extended practice on these types of sounds are necessary to ensure accurate decoding and encoding.

The developmental progression of phonological and phonemic awareness

There are two dimensions of phonemic awareness that we can examine through a developmental lens. One developmental dimension, outlined by Louisa Moats in *Teaching Reading is Rocket Science* (1999), focuses on the knowledge base that teachers need to have in order to teach phonological and phonemic awareness. Using the analogy of a rocket ship, let's look at three levels of phonological awareness that move students' awareness of word structure from larger to smaller units of speech.

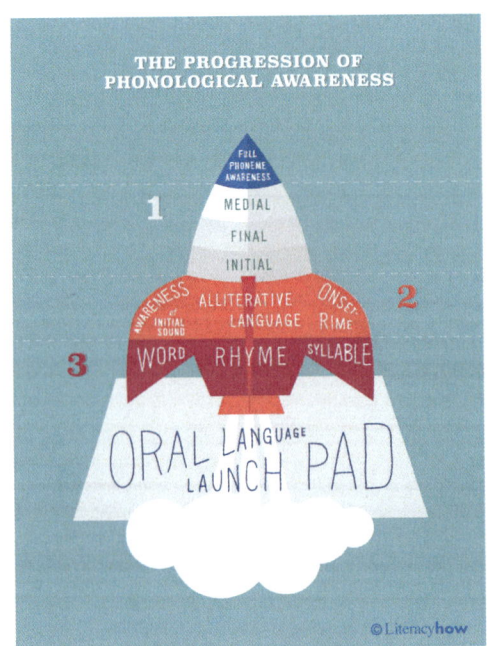

Level 3 of the rocket ship represents the largest units of sound. Initially instruction can capitalize on students' oral language by having them count the number of words in a spoken sentence. For example, *I love school* (3 words). Next, instruction can focus on rhyme, including both rhyme recognition (e.g., Do **sock** and **rock** rhyme?) and rhyme production (e.g., Say a word that rhymes with **sock**. (**rock**)) Both skills require an awareness that rhyming words have the same vowel and consonant sound at the end of the words. The last unit in level 3 focuses on syllable awareness. Syllables are units of speech containing one vowel sound. Because a vowel is an open sound, the chin drops as the mouth opens; therefore, students can learn to count the number of syllables by counting the number of times the chin drops. This kinesthetic input can be helpful for students who have difficulty hearing syllables in words. Instruction in syllable segmentation should include both segmenting into syllable units (e.g., What are the syllables in the name **Jessica**? *Jess- i – ca*.) and blending them back together (e.g., *Jess- i – ca* = **Jessica**). Playing with large units of speech lays the foundation and primes the brain's listening center so that it can process smaller units of sound.

In Level 2 of the rocket ship, instruction moves to initial sound awareness, alliteration, and onset rime. The first step is to develop an awareness of the first sound in words. For this instruction, select words that begin with continuant sounds, that is sounds that can be drawn out or elongated until the speaker runs out of breath (e.g., / s /, / m /, / f /). Equally important is to avoid using words with consonant blends (e.g., **st**, **fl**) because blends are so closely co-articulated that the component sounds are difficult to perceive. For example, the / s / in **sun** is much easier to perceive than the / s / in **stick**. Alliteration, the repetition of words that begin with the same initial sound as in *Peter Piper picked a peck of pickled peppers*, further builds students' awareness of initial sounds. Once students gain proficiency with initial sounds, they are ready to segment words into their onset (i.e., initial sounds) and rime (i.e., the vowel and the consonant sounds that follow the vowel). For example, **fat** is composed of the onset **f** and rime **at**. Once students can segment and blend onsets and rimes, they are ready for the last level of phonological awareness, which is phonemic awareness.

Level 1 brings students to full segmentation and blending of the sounds (phonemes) in words. Phonemic segmentation is the ability to identify the sounds in a one-syllable unit (i.e., a whole word **cat** or part of a word **cat** in **cattle**). The word **cat** is segmented into / k / / ă / / t /. Phonemic blending is the ability to put the sounds back together into a syllable or word (i.e., / k / / ă / / t / = **cat**). The most advanced phase of phoneme awareness is referred to as manipulation. Phoneme manipulation requires students to substitute (e.g., change **mat** to **sat**), add (e.g., say **lip** and add / f / to make **flip**) or delete (e.g., say **mat** without the / m / to make **at**) sounds in words. At Level 1 of the rocket ship analogy, students also learn the impact that changing a single phoneme in a word has on meaning. Changing p**o**t to p**e**t (i.e., changing the vowel from **o** to **e**) changes the meaning from something to cook with to an animal that lives in your home.

The other developmental dimension frames the progression in terms of the age at which typically developing children are able to do the necessary phonemic analyses tasks. For teachers, this developmental context is important to know and understand in order to sequence tasks appropriately and to set expectations realistically. The following table presents this information chronologically from early awareness of rhyming up to the most sophisticated and complex phoneme manipulation tasks involving deletion (e.g., "Say **snail**. Say it again, without the /n/.")

Ages at which 80-90 percent of typical students have achieved a phonological skill

Age	Skill Domain	Sample Tasks
4	Rote imitation and enjoyment of rhyme and alliteration	**pool, drool, tool** "Seven silly snakes sang songs seriously."
5	Rhyme recognition, odd word out	"Which two words rhyme: **stair, steel, chair**?"
	Recognition of phonemic changes in words	"*Hickory Dickory Clock*. That's not right!"
	Clapping, counting syllables	**truck** (1 syllable) **airplane** (2 syllables) **boat** (1 syllable) **automobile** (4 syllables)
5½	Distinguishing and remembering separate phonemes in a series	Show sequences of single phonemes with colored blocks: /s/ /s/ /f/; /z/ /sh/ /z/.
	Blending onset and rime	"What word?" **th-umb** **qu-een** **h-ope**
	Producing a rhyme	"Tell me a word that rhymes with **car**." (**star**)
	Matching initial sounds; isolating an initial sound	"Say the first sound in **ride** (/r/); **sock** (/s/); **love** (/l/)."
6	Compound word deletion	"Say **cowboy**. Say it again, but don't say **cow**."
	Syllable deletion	"Say **parsnip**. Say it again, but don't say **par**."
	Blending of two and three phonemes	/z/ /ū/ (**zoo**) /sh/ /ŏ/ /p/ (**shop**) /h/ /ou/ /s/ (**house**)

	Phoneme segmentation of words that have simple syllables with two or three phonemes (no blends)	"Say the word as you move a chip for each sound." **sh-e** **m-a-n** **l-e-g**
6½	Phoneme segmentation of words that have up to three or four phonemes (include blends)	"Say the word slowly while you tap the sounds." **b-a-ck** **ch-ee-se** **c-l-ou-d**
	Phoneme substitution to build new words that have simple syllables (no blends)	"Change the /j/ in **cage** to /n/. Change the /ā/ in **cane** to /ō/."
7	Sound deletion (initial and final positions)	"Say **meat**. Say it again, without the /m/." "Say **safe**. Say it again, without the /f/."
8	Sound deletion (initial position, include blends)	"Say **prank**. Say it again, without the /p/."
9	Sound deletion (medial and final blend positions)	"Say **snail**. Say it again, without the /n/." "Say **fork**. Say it again, without the /k/."

From http://www.readingrockets.org/article/development-phonological-skills

Features of effective instructional practices

Researchers have identified effective practices to teach literacy concepts and skills. Let's see how these practices apply to phonemic awareness instruction.

- **Explicit instruction**: Explicit instruction means direct teaching of content, strategies and skills. In terms of phonemic awareness, explicit instruction focuses on the individual sound structure of spoken words. For example, phonemic awareness includes skills such as recognizing words that rhyme (e.g., **cat** and **bat** rhyme; **cat** and **cab** do not), identifying the beginning sound in a word (e.g., What is the first sound in **mat**? (/ m /), segmenting spoken words into the individual sounds (e.g., What are the sounds in mat? (/ m / / a / / t /). (See the activities **Onset-Rime Awareness** page 22 and **Say It and Move It** page 28.)

- **Emphasis on making abstract concepts concrete**: Multisensory techniques—including tangible objects, visuals, graphics and color coding and kinesthetic techniques—help to make abstract concepts concrete. For example, the use of blocks to represent each sound in a spoken word and clapping for each word in a sentence make abstract language elements more tangible and accessible. (See the activities **Picture/Sound Sort** page 19 and **Going on a Trip** page 26.)

- **Emphasis on automaticity**: Automaticity helps overcome a key obstacle to learning—the limited capacity of working memory. The goal of phonemic awareness instruction is for students to segment sounds in words and blend sounds automatically. Automatic segmentation transfers to encoding (spelling) and blending transfers to decoding (reading).

- **Development of meta-cognitive strategies**: Meta-cognitive strategies focus on the awareness or analysis of what one is learning. In the case of phonemic awareness, this awareness and analysis is a metalinguistic skill that teaches students to consciously think about the internal sound structure of words, which is foundational to learning phonics. For example, the ability to combine—or blend—a sequence of sounds into a word is essential to apply the alphabetic principle to read words. Practice listening to a sequence of speech sounds and blending them into a word is one of these critical skills. (See the activity **Aliens from Outer Space** page 32.)

- **Stress on cumulative, systematic, and sequential presentation of content and skills**: The foundation of English—such as its sounds, syllable, and structures—should be presented in a logical order. In the case of phonological development, there is a clear developmental progression from words, to syllables, to onset-rime patterns, and finally to phonemes. (See section "The developmental progression of phonological and phonemic awareness" page 10.)

- **Use of data to guide instruction**: Evidence of learning—be it identifying the correct number of phonemes in a spoken word or accurately blending a sequence of sounds into a word—provides critical data to inform the focus and pacing of instruction. Additionally, performance data from screening tools (e.g., DIBELS, AIMSweb, easyCBM) indicate whether or not students are on the necessary trajectory to be skilled decoders by third grade.

Cognitive preparation for text utilization for phonemic awareness instruction

Cognitive preparation, the intentional act of utilizing content knowledge in lesson preparation, allows teachers to view text through the lens of particular phonological or phonemic awareness tasks. In the case of phonemic awareness, that knowledge includes isolation of initial sounds in words, segmentation of words by phoneme in spoken words and blending spoken sounds into a word. As with any text-based application, students must first learn the phonological or phonemic content through direct and explicit instruction, which is the goal of the activities in this domain. Once students can demonstrate these skills through explicit instruction, teachers can provide ongoing practice and application through predetermined use of text selections.

At times a poem or book will inspire a particular kind of word play based on alliteration or a rhyming refrain. For example, the poem *Hickory, Dickory Dock* provides a playful rhyming pattern to practice recognizing words that rhyme. Once students have learned how words rhyme—namely the rime stays the same but the onset changes—poems offer a readymade source to see rhyming in action. After reading the poem, students are prepared to understand why **dock** and **clock** rhyme and why **clock** and **one** don't. This understanding enhances the anticipation and enjoyment of poetry that rhymes.

> Hickory Dickory dock
> The mouse ran up the clock,
> The clock struck one
> The mouse ran down,
> Hickory Dickory dock.

Other times, we can use children's stories to select vocabulary to practice a particular syllable or phoneme manipulation task. For example, the classic story *Goldilocks and the Three Bears* is rich with vocabulary with differing numbers of syllables. Once students have learned how to determine the number of syllables in words, we can use words from the story to practice pronunciation of words with differing numbers of syllables, such as **bear** (1), **porridge** (2) and **Goldilocks** (3).

 **ACTIVITIES for Instruction and Informal Assessment**

The activities in this section focus on the manipulation of parts and sounds in words as the basis for acquiring the alphabetic principle, the term used for the relationship between the sounds of spoken language (phonemes) and the letters of written language (graphemes). The activities in the phonemic awareness domain involve:

- Isolation—identify a position-specific sound within a word (e.g., what's the first sound in / *ball* /? / *b* /); discriminate, match, and sort pictures, words and/or objects according to a targeted sound or pattern (e.g., Which words begin with the sound / *m* /? **m**onster, puppy, **m**oon)
- Onset-Rime Awareness: Which word rhymes with / *kat* /? **hat**, ham, cap)
- Segmentation—break a word into its syllables or sound (phonemes) parts (e.g., What are the syllables in / *sunset* /? / *sun* / / *set* /; What are the sounds in / *sun* /? / s / / ŭ / / n /)
- Blending—combine a sequence of syllables or sounds (phonemes) into a word (e.g., Listen: / *base* / / *ball* /. What's the word? / *baseball* /; Listen: / b / / ă / / t /. What's the word? / *bat* /?)

The activities in this domain include:

	Stage 0	Stage 1	Stage 2
Instruction	\multicolumn{3}{c}{Isolation (See page 18)}	
	Picture/Sound Sort (Identify phonemes at various positions in words)	Mirror Mouth (Produce phonemes accurately)	
	\multicolumn{3}{c}{Onset-Rime Awareness (See page 22)}	
	Odd One Out (Determine if labels for pictures or objects rhyme)		
	That's Nonsense (Identify and produce rhyming words)		
	\multicolumn{3}{c}{Segmentation (See page 25)}	
	Going on a Trip (Segment words into syllables)	Say It and Move It (Segment words into phonemes)	
	\multicolumn{3}{c}{Blending (See page 31)}	
		Aliens from Outer Space (Blend phonemes into words)	

	Stage 0	Stage 1	Stage 2
Informal Assessment	The following links are suggested as the kinds of assessments that are available to evaluate children's phonemic awareness skills. They are provided as examples and are not intended to be exhaustive. Readers are also encouraged to explore the assessments included as part of published programs that they use or through local and state assessment systems. CORE Introduction to Assessing Reading http://www.academictherapy.com/pdfs/multiMeasures.pdf Building RTI – University of Texas at Austin Spanish Phonemic Awareness Test http://buildingrti.utexas.org/lessons/phonological-awareness-spanish-segmenting-and-blending-activitycenter Scholastic Phonemic Awareness Assessment http://samresources.scholastic.com/ResourceManager/previewresource.spr?_page=0&objectId=15422		

Isolation

The following activities focus on isolating phonemes in various positions in words, as well as their accurate speech production

Domain: Phonemic Awareness

Background information for this activity:

Phoneme isolation, that is the ability to identify a sound in a specific position in a word, is a critical phoneme awareness skill to read and spell words. Being able to identify a sound in a targeted position, such as "What's the first sound in / *ball* /?" is foundational to rhyme production, matching words with pictures or other words with the same beginning sound, and spelling words. (See **Picture/Sound Sort** activity page 19.)

English is made up of 44 speech sounds. In order to read and spell words, it is essential for students to accurately produce these speech sounds. (See **Mirror Mouth** activity page 21.) Sounds in English fit into two distinct categories—consonant and vowels. Consonant sounds stop, block or squeeze the air as we say them. In contrast, vowel sounds do not obstruct the flow of air as we say them. Multisensory techniques, such as kinesthetic feedback, visual feedback, and oral-motor distinctions, are helpful in guiding students to make and distinguish the sounds of English.

Stage 0	Stage 1	Stage 2
Picture/Sound Sort • Use pictures representing targeted phonemes	Mirror Mouth • Develop speech sound production	

Isolation: Picture/Sound Sort (Stage 0)

Objective: To isolate and identify phonemes in various positions in words (i.e., initial, final, medial)

Target students: Pre-K – K

Materials needed: Pocket chart to display pictures, set of pictures with targeted sounds

How to do the activity:

1. Determine the initial, final or medial sounds[1,2] that you want students to isolate and identify.
2. Set up pocket chart with header pictures (i.e., pictures that are key words for the targeted sounds). For example, to practice discriminating the initial sounds / b / and / p /, the header pictures could be a **ball** and a **pig**.

3. Present selected pictures for the sort one at a time. Ask students to name the pictured object and/or repeat[3] the word after you.

4. Have students compare the targeted sound (initial, final or medial) to the header pictures. Place the picture under the header that matches the targeted sound. For example, a picture of a bear

would be sorted under **ball** because **bear** begins with the same sound as **ball**; a picture of a **pumpkin** would be sorted under **pig** because **pumpkin** begins with the same sound as **pig**.

5. Continue with the remaining pictures. Encourage students to reflect on their choices.

6. After sorting all of the pictures, have students name the pictures in each category. Have students isolate and stress the sound in the targeted position to confirm they have placed the pictures in the correct category.

Tips for Teaching

[1] Use the sequence of intial sound, final sound and medial sound to plan instruction. Of special note is the importance of spending time on the final sound. Final sounds are difficult to isolate even with meticulous pronunciation because in running speech, we often drop the ends of words.

[2] Begin by contrasting two sounds to ensure mastery before adding others. Sort by sound and make sure that each picture is compared to the header with the "key" word/picture. As children gain proficiency, add an oddball category, that is a category for words that don't fit the targeted sounds.

[3] Whenever you do phonemic awareness work, it's important to articulate words very clearly and also ensure that children are always repeating the words so that you can check to make sure that they're pronouncing the word accurately.

Isolation: Mirror Mouth (Stage 1)

Objective: To practice accurate phoneme pronunciation

Target students: Pre-K – K

Materials needed: individual handheld mirrors

How to do the activity:

Sounds in English fit into two distinct categories—consonant and vowels. Consonant sounds stop, block or squeeze the air as we say them. In contrast, vowel sounds do not obstruct the flow of air as we say them. Multisensory techniques are helpful in guiding students to make and distinguish the sounds of English. These techniques include

- Kinesthetic feedback: For example, we can do the "chin drop check" to help decide if a sound is a consonant or a vowel. Our chin doesn't drop when we make a consonant sound. Try it with / k /, / g /, / d /, and / s /. Our chin does drop when we say a vowel sound. Try it with / ŏ / as in **octopus** and / ă / as in **apple**.
- Visual feedback: Handheld mirrors make it possible for students to observe the position of the articulators—lips, teeth and tongue—while making specific sounds.
- Motor distinctions: As we go through the various sounds, we will explore voiced and unvoiced pairs where sounds share the same mouth movements, but one is voiced (motor on – voice box vibrates) and one is unvoiced (motor off – voice box still). Students feel their throats to see if their voice (motor) is on or off (feel the buzz of a bee or not- reference to picture).
Voiced/unvoiced pairs may be referred to as "the noisy and quiet brothers" to help students make a connection.

For example, for the consonant pair / p / and / b /,

- Use mirrors or have students look at the teacher's mouth as she makes the sound. Have students discover that the mouth formation is the same for each sound.
- Have students feel the puff of air released on the back of their hand for the unvoiced sounds / p / because more air escapes with a voiceless sound.
- Have students feel their throats for voiced and unvoiced sounds.
- Ask them to look at their mouths and describe what is happening. What part of their mouth is moving?
- Be sure students do not drop their chins when making these sounds to avoid adding the / ŭ / to the consonant sound.

Repeat with other consonant pairs: / f / and / v /; / t / and / d /; / s / and / z /.

Onset-Rime Awareness

The following rhyming activities focuses on the recognition of word pairs that rhyme.

Domain: Phonemic Awareness

Objective: To identify words that rhyme

Background information for these activities:

Words that rhyme share a common sound pattern—the vowel and what comes after it. This is called the rime component of a word (e.g., the –at in **bat**; -ing in **sting**; -ark in **bark**). Recognizing words that rhyme requires the ability to manipulate sounds in words, specifically the sound(s) before the rime (i.e., the onset). Words that rhyme sound the same at the end; the first phoneme(s) changes to create words that rhyme (e.g., **cat**, **bat**, **flat**, **chat**). Rhyming requires the ability to isolate an initial sound(s) and substitute another sound(s) while keeping the rime the same.

Producing words that rhyme requires the ability to isolate an initial sound(s) and substitute another sound(s) while keeping the rime the same. For example, to produce a word that rhymes with **book**, students must isolate the initial sound (/ *b* /), substitute another sound (e.g., / *l* /) and combine it with the rime component (/ *ook* /). The new word that rhymes is **look**. Due to these multiple phoneme manipulations, production of rhyming words is more difficult than recognition of words that rhyme. Practice both recognizing and generating rhyming words increases phonemic awareness, an ability critical to learn to read. (See **Odd One Out** and **That's Nonsense** activities pages 23 and 24.)

Stage 0	Stage 1	Stage 2
Odd One Out • Sets of pictures or objects representing words that rhyme That's Nonsense • Sets of objects to prompt rhyming words		

Onset-Rime Awareness: Odd One Out (Stage 0)

Objective: To identify words that rhyme[1,2]

Target students: Pre-K – K

Materials needed: Sets of objects or pictures representing words that rhyme (or words that have the same initial or final sound) with one item that does not rhyme (e.g., car, star, jar, book).

How to do activity:
1. Place set of objects or pictures in the middle of a circle so all students can see them.

2. Name the objects and have students repeat the name of each object for accurate phonological representation.
3. Sing: "One of these things is not like the others, one of these things just doesn't belong. Can you guess which thing is not like the others before the end of the song?" After students guess, say: "**Car, star, jar** rhyme. **Book** doesn't because it doesn't sound the same at the end. It doesn't rhyme. Let's practice saying the rhyming words again!"
4. Repeat with another set of objects.

Tips for Teaching

[1] This activity can be adapted for other phonological or phonemic skills. For example, to focus on initial sound isolation, use a set of objects or pictures to identify a word that does not have the same initial sound (e.g., milk, mouse, man, *sun*). The same approach can be used for final sound isolation (e.g., fin, man, *duck*, pan).

[2] When doing **Odd One Out** to practice isolation of initial or final sounds, begin with continuant sounds (i.e., / s /, / m /, / f /), because students can stretch these sounds out more easily than they can with a stop sound (i.e., / p /, / t /, / g /).

Onset-Rime Awareness: That's Nonsense (Stage 0)

Objective: To identify and produce words that rhyme

Target students: Pre-K – K

Materials needed: Preplanned list of classroom objects such as **desk, chair, rug, cubby, book, pencil,** and **paper**; hand puppet with movable mouth; other sets of objects, such as pretend fruits, animals, and vehicles

How to do activity:

1. Tell students that a new teacher has come to teach at their school. Introduce the hand puppet as Ms./Mr. Nonsense. The only problem is that s/he speaks "nonsense."
2. Have students listen to Ms./Mr. Nonsense to help them figure out the English words that rhyme with nonsense words their new teacher uses.
3. Use the puppet to "say" the words as Ms./Mr. Nonsense gives the directions. For example, "Children, place your hands on top of your 'nesks.'" Model your thought process by thinking aloud: "Nesks sounds like 'desks,' Oh, Ms./Mr. Nonsense must want us to place our hands on top of our 'desks'." Have students repeat both the nonsense and real words to reinforce hearing and saying the rhyming pair of words themselves.
4. Continue with other examples, such as: "Children, put our backpacks in your 'wubby,' (cubby)"; "Write your name on the top of your 'maper,' (paper); and so on.
5. Continue to give nonsensical directions until you observe that students are able to recognize rhyme.
6. Give students a turn being Ms./Mr. Nonsense to practice producing rhymes. Have student "teachers" give directions to the rest of the class.
7. Repeat the activity using other sets of objects, such as the pretend fruits, animals, and vehicles for additional practice.

Note: The book, *The Hungry Thing* by Jan Slepian (2001), was the inspiration for this activity.

Segmentation

The following activities focus on segmenting words into syllable or phoneme units.

Domain: Phonological and Phonemic Awareness

Objective: To segment words into syllables or phoneme units

Background information for this activity:

Syllable segmentation is an important phonological awareness skill that requires breaking a spoken word into its syllable components. (See **Going on a Trip** activity page 26.) Syllables are structured around a vowel sound; the number of vowel sounds in a word determines the number of syllables (e.g., **me** = 1; **hobo** = 2; **fantastic** = 3, and so on). A syllable can be composed of a single vowel, such as the word "I" or the first syllable in the word *able*. Usually, a syllable is made up of a combination of consonants and vowels. These consonant and vowel patterns can be categorized into six syllable patterns: closed, open, silent e, vowel teams, R-controlled, and consonant-le. (Refer to **Syllable Inspectors** in *Phonics: Knowledge to Practice* in the Literacy How Professional Learning series for more information about the six syllable patterns.)

The ability to segment—or break—a word into its sequence of speech sounds is critically important to becoming an accurate speller. Segmentation requires the listener to identify the sequence of sounds in a word. For example, when presented with the word **fast**, the listener responds with the sounds / f / / ă / / s / / t /. This is the underlying phonemic awareness ability needed to encode, that is spell, a spoken word. (See **Say It and Move It** activity page 28.)

Stage 0	Stage 1	Stage 2
Going on a Trip • Objects and pictures representing words with different numbers of syllables	Say It and Move It[1] • Words with two, three, four and five phonemes	

[1]Adapted from Blachman, B.A., Ball, E.W., Black, R., & Tangel, D. M. (2000) *Road to the Code: A Phonological Awareness Program for Young Children*. Brookes Publishing: Baltimore, MD.

Segmentation: Going on a Trip (Stage 0)

Objective: To segment words into syllables.

Target students: Pre-K – K

Materials needed: Three boxes as pretend suitcases each one marked with one, two, or three dots; a set of objects or pictures of things that you might take on a trip (e.g., socks, pajamas, toothbrush, blanket, pillow) [1]

How to do the activity:

1. Display the pictures and/or objects of things you might take on a trip. Name each object and have students repeat the names for accurate pronunciation.
2. Name one of the objects or pictures again (e.g., toothbrush). Clap once for each syllable in the word. Ask: "How many time did we clap?" (2) Have students repeat the word **toothbrush** a couple times. Clap for each syllable (i.e., tooth/brush) as the students say the word with you.
3. Repeat with other pictures and/or objects (e.g., socks, pajamas, pillow) to be sure the students understand the task.[2]
4. Practice: Display three suitcases, each labeled with dots and a picture of an object representing words with the designated number of syllables: one (**book**), two (**hairbrush**) or three (**pajamas**)

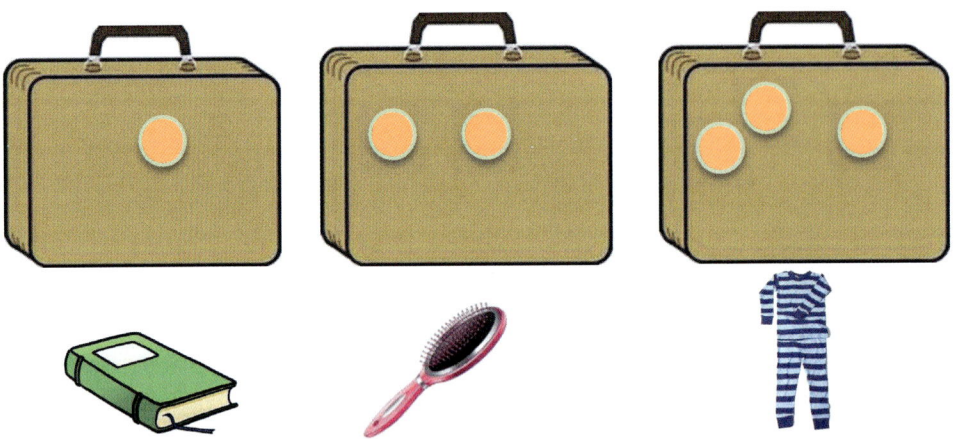

   a. Point to the suitcase with the **book** in it. Have students name the object (**book**), clap as they say the word, and tell how many times they clapped (*one time*).
   b. Continue with the suitcase with the **hairbrush** in it. Have students name the object (**hairbrush**), clap as they say the word—once for each syllable, and tell how many times they clapped (*two times*).

c. Finally, point to the suitcase with the **pajamas** in it. Have students name the object (**pajamas**), clap as they say the word—once for each syllable, and tell how many times they clapped (*three times*).
5. Present the other pictures or objects. For each object, have students name the object, clap once for each syllable as they say the name, and tell how many times they clapped. Place each object in the suitcase that matches the number of syllables in the name.
6. Continue with all of the objects. Sort them by the number of syllables in their names. Make sure that all children are repeating the words and clapping the number of syllables.

Tips for Teaching

[1]This activity can be adapted with other categories of objects that might be carried in other containers. For example, grocery bags with items that that you purchase at the grocery store (e.g., eggs, milk, cookies, tomatoes, bread, popsicles, and so on) or tool boxes with items that you keep in the box (e.g., nails, hammer, saw, screws, pliers, ruler, and so on).

[2]If students have difficulty synchronizing the claps with the syllables in the word, show them how to place one of their hands under their chin to "feel the syllables" each time their chin touches their hand. Each touch equals a syllable.

Segmentation: Say It and Move It (Stage 1)

Objective: To practice segmenting one syllable words with 1-5 sounds

Target students: K – 2

Materials needed: Say It and Move It boards (one for each student)[1], tokens; list of words with two, three, four or five phonemes

How to do activity:

1. Provide each student with a Say It and Move It board and with the number of tokens corresponding to the number of phonemes in the words on the list.[2, 3, 4, 5] Have students place the tokens in the box on their Say It and Move It board.

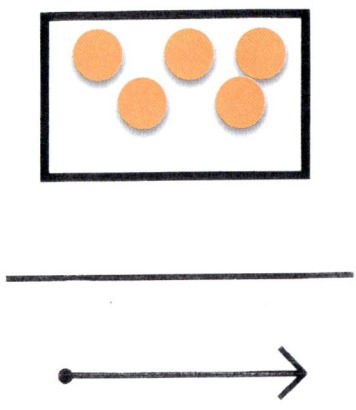

2. Model the procedure as follows:
    a. Place tokens in the box on your Say It and Move It board.
    b. Say a word on the list (e.g., **me**)
    c. Move one token from the box to the line for each sound in the word (move one token for / m / and another for / ē /)

28

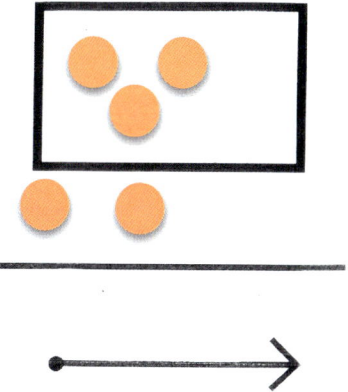

   d. Identify the number of sounds in the word (2)
   e. Point to each token and say the sound that corresponds from the word (/ m / / ē /)
   f. Say the word (**me**)
   g. Repeat steps with another word to model the procedure for students.
3. Use the following prompts to have students do the Say It and Move it procedure with you.
   a. "Repeat after me ____ (say word from the list) ____." (Students repeat word.)
   b. "Say it and move it." (Students move a token from the box to the line for each sound in the word.)
   c. "How many sounds in (say word)?" (Students respond.)
   d. "Point and say the sounds." (Students say sounds in word.)
   e. "Say the word." (Students say the word.)
4. Continue with other words on the list. Check that students are pronouncing the word correctly and synchronizing saying the sounds as they move each token. Provide additional modeling of the task and immediate corrective feedback.

Tips for Teaching

[1] A sample Say It and Move It board is provided in the Appendix page 126.

[2] Initially provide the same number of tokens as phonemes in the word. As students become more proficient, challenge students by providing more tokens than required for the number of phonemes in the word.

[3] Follow the scope and sequence of sound/spelling associations used by the teacher, school or district. Doing this reinforces the sounds and ensures greater accuracy in doing the task. Within that scope and sequence, it is most effective to start with continuant sounds (e.g., / m /, / s /, / ă /).

[4] Start small. Begin with single sounds and sequence of single sounds and build to two-phoneme words (e.g., / me /, / sew /, / knee /). Do not be fooled by the written spelling of the word. For example, while the word **knee** has four letters **k** – **n** – **e** – **e**, there are only two sounds (phonemes) in the word - / n / / ē /.

[5] When moving to more difficult sound sequences, such as words containing initial or final consonant combinations (i.e., blends), develop the sound segmentation skill by building from the rime. For example, begin with the rime (e.g., / ŏp /), add a consonant (e.g., / *top* /), and end with another consonant (e.g., / *stop* /). This approach is termed building from the "inside out." As students gain skill with blends this way, move to practice with blends building from the "outside in." For example, begin with / ăn /, add a consonant (e.g., / *pan* /), and end by inserting another consonant (e.g., / *plan* /).

Blending

The following activity focuses on combining (blending) a sequence of spoken sounds into a word.

Domain: Phonemic Awareness

Objective: To blend sounds into words.

Background information for this activity:

The ability to combine—or blend—a sequence of speech sounds into a word is critically important to decoding and becoming a fluent reader. Sound blending requires the listener to hold a sequence of sounds in working memory long enough to combine them accurately into a word. For example, when presented with the following sequence of speech sounds / *sh* / / *ĭ* / / *p* /, the listener responds with the word **ship**. (See **Aliens from Outer Space** activity page 32.) The ability to blend sounds into a word facilitates using knowledge of sound-letter associations to decode words in print.

Stage 0	Stage 1	Stage 2
	Aliens from Outer Space • Words with two, three, four and five phonemes	

Blending: Aliens from Outer Space (Stage 1)

Objective: To blend sounds into words

Target students: K – 2

Materials needed: Word bank; picture of an alien or alien figure

How to do the activity:

1. Tell students that friendly creatures called aliens from outer space came to earth. These creatures have a different way of talking. For example, for **cake** they say / k / / ā / / k /. For **dog** they say / d / / aw / / g /.
2. Tell students that you will say a word the way the aliens do, they have to say it the way humans (we) say it.
3. Explain that you are going to talk like the aliens. When you do, you will use the following hand gesture: Start with your hands together in front of you and move them apart as you break apart the word into its component sounds. Demonstrate with the word mom: "The aliens say / m / / ŏ / / m /."
4. Tell students they will say the word the way we (humans) do. When you demonstrate saying the word, bring your hands together and clap. "We say / mom /." [1]
5. Continue with additional words from the word bank[2, 3]. Repeat hand gestures each time you deliver a word sound-by-sound and as you put the word back together.
    - "The aliens say / s / / ŭ / / n /." We say, ____/ sun /_____."
    - "The aliens say / ch / / ĭ / / n /." We say, ____/ chin /_____."

Tips for Teaching

[1] Students should only say the target word; that is the word rather than the sequence of sounds. To prompt students to say the word say, "We say, _____(students say the target word)_____."

[2] Words selected for this activity should follow the scope and sequence of sound/spelling associations used by the teacher, school or district. Doing this reinforces the sounds and ensures greater accuracy in doing the task.

[3] Factors impacting the level of task difficulty are word length and the duration between the presentation of sounds (i.e. the longer the pause between each sound, the more difficult it will be to blend the sounds back together).

Text Selection Skills Analyses

Any text selection provides opportunities for teachers to help students apply content, skills and strategies. In the case of the phonemic awareness domain, the use of text provides opportunities to increase awareness of the phoneme structure of words.

To take advantage of these opportunities, teachers must first consider what students have *already* learned through direct and explicit instruction. This surface level learning is a prerequisite in order for students to transfer this learning to text (Fisher, Frey & Hattie, 2016). Next teachers need to analyze text to determine what opportunities exist for students to practice and apply content, skills and strategies acquired through direct instruction. This requires that teachers preview the text to identify the domain-specific content (e.g., phonemic awareness) that can be reinforced when reading the text selection. The use of text selections requires consideration of what students have been taught previously and what they have learned, as well as the skill requirements needed to read the selection. This analytical process is called cognitive preparation during which teachers must consider the match between what students know (i.e., content, skills and strategies) and the demands of the task (e.g., phonemic awareness) so their students can access and master the meaning of the text.

In this section of *Phonemic Awareness: Knowledge to Practice*, we model this process with a series of different texts. For each text selection, we provide a **Text Analysis** table with examples of domain-specific learning objectives that are applicable for the selection. The table provides learning objectives for multiple domains to illustrate the range of options in using a text selection. The table of objectives also demonstrates that it is possible to integrate several aspects of literacy development through strategic use of the same text selection. Following the objectives, we draw from activities in the **Activities for Instruction and Informal Assessment** section to show how to tailor the activities to the text selection. The **Activity Application to Text** table includes a "Think Aloud" component in which we offer an example of the thinking that should occur to make a match between what students know and what the text offers for skill application to foster the development of phonemic awareness. The **Text Analyses** examples are presented in the order of the activities on pages 16.

Stage 0

A Trip to the Zoo

My grandmother took me to the zoo on a Saturday in May.
I had so much fun walking around, watching the animals at play!

The colors and sounds, they did abound, as we ambled around the zoo.
I saw so many wonderful sights, some familiar and some brand new.

One colorful peacock spread his feathers beneath a lotus tree.
Two chatty monkeys hung from a branch while they fixed their eyes on me.

Three striped zebras nibbled hay that was scattered upon the ground.
Four lazy lions roamed with their pride but didn't make a sound.

Five elephants played next to a river spraying water oh so far!
And six young cubs slept beside their mother, a bear the color of tar.

Seven giraffes stood in a herd, necks stretching towards the sky.
Eight beady eyes peered from their perch, four owls that didn't fly.

A troop of nine gorillas played and played behind the bars so tall.
And last but not least, ten sea lions swam in a pool and played ball.

As we left the zoo I thanked gramma for spending the day with me.
And I let her know about my plan. A zookeeper I shall be!

Text Analysis

Alphabetic Principle	Vocabulary/Syntax	Comprehension
• Synchromesh: Finger point while reciting the poem • Letter knowledge: Recognize and name letters • Phonological Awareness: Rhyme recognition using words that end with the same sound (e.g., May, play; zoo, new; tree, me)	• Discuss words from the poem that may be unfamiliar (sip, munch, yummy) • Read in meaningful grammatical phrases	Ask literal and inferential questions

Activity Application to Text

Lesson development "Think Aloud"	Lesson Focus: Phonemic Awareness – Rhyme recognition
	Activity: Odd One Out (See page 23)
	Group size: Small Group
Poetry that includes rhyming words is a natural medium for working on rhyme recognition. The activity **Odd One Out** can be used as a warm up to remind students about how words rhyme. Words from *A Trip to the Zoo* provide multiple examples to practice rhyme recognition.	Materials needed: Sets of pictures representing words that have the same final sound with one item that does not have the same final sound (e.g., tree, bee, three, ball); *A Trip to the Zoo* written on poster paper or a white board. How to do activity: 1. Place pictures in the middle of a circle so all students can see them. 2. Name the pictures and have students repeat the name of each one for accurate phonological representation. 3. Sing: "One of these things is not like the others, one of these things just doesn't belong. Can you guess which thing is not like the others before the end of the song?" After students guess, say: "tree, bee, and three have the same sound at the end - / ē /. These words rhyme. Ball doesn't belong because it doesn't have the same sound at the end. Let's practice saying words that end with the same sound again!" 4. Display the poem, *A Trip to the Zoo*. Read the first stanza. Ask: What sound do **May** and **play** end with? (/ ā /) 5. Continue with remaining stanzas of the poem asking students to listen for the words that end with the same sound (e.g., **zoo** and **new** - / oo /; **far** and **tar** - / ar /; **sky** and **fly** - / ī /; **me** and **be** - / ē /). 6. End the lesson by naming the words that have the same ending sound: **May** and **play**; **zoo** and **new**; **far** and **tar**; **sky** and **fly**; and **me** and **be**.

Stage 0

The Hungry Girl[1]

"I'm hungry!"
Said the little girl
To her dearest dad
"Would you like to sip some soup?
That's what your brother had."

"No! I'm hungry!"
Said the little girl
To her dearest dad
"Would you like to taste this toast?
That's what your brother had."

"No! I'm hungry!"
Said the little girl
To her dearest dad
"Would you like to munch a muffin?
That's what your brother had."

No! I'm hungry!"
Said the little girl
To her dearest dad
"Would you like some yummy yogurt?
That's not what your brother had."

"Yes I would!"
Said the little girl
To her dearest dad
She ate the yogurt by herself,
Which made her brother mad!

Text Analysis

Alphabetic Principle	Vocabulary/Syntax	Comprehension
- Synchromesh: Finger point while reciting the poem - Letter knowledge: Recognize and name letters - Phonological Awareness: Initial phoneme isolation and identification using alliterative words (**sip, some, soup; taste, toast; munch, muffin; yummy, yogurt**)	- Discuss words from the poem that may be unfamiliar (sip, munch, yummy) - Read in meaningful grammatical phrases	Ask literal and inferential questions

Activity Application to Text

Lesson development "Think Aloud"	Lesson Focus: Phoneme Awareness – Initial phoneme isolation and identification
	Activity: Picture/Sound Sort (See page 19)
	Group size: Small Group
Alliterative poetry is a natural medium for working on initial sound awareness. The activity **Picture/Sound Sort** can be used as a warm up to isolate and identify the initial sound in the words in *The Hungry Girl*.	Materials needed: Sets of objects or pictures representing initial sounds for targeted words in the poem (e.g., seal for / s /, monkey for / m /, tiger for / t /, yak for / y /); *The Hungry Girl* written on poster paper or a white board.

How to do activity:
1. Place set of objects or pictures in the middle of a circle so all students can see them.
2. Name the objects and have students repeat the name of each object for accurate phonological representation.
3. Present the pictures representing the targeted initial sounds (e.g., seal for / s /, monkey for / m /, tiger for / t /, yak for / y /)
4. Display the poem, *The Hungry Girl*. Read the first stanza. Ask: What sound do **sip** and **soup** begin with? (/ s /)
5. Continue with remaining stanzas of the poem asking students to listen for the words that begin with the same sound. (e.g., **taste** and **toast** - / t /; **munch** and **muffin** - / m /; **yummy** and **yogurt** - / y /)
6. End the lesson by writing the words with the same initial sound on the poster paper or on the white board. Have students think of other words that start with the same sounds and write them in a list. For example, under the words **sip** and **soup**, you might add **sun**, **silly**, and **sock**.
7. Read the words in each list emphasizing that they all begin with the same sound. For the words **sip**, **soup**, **sun**, **silly**, and **sock**, the initial sound is / s /. |

[1] Go to www.ReadWorks.org for a printable version of *The Hungry Girl*

Stage 1

This Red Sled[2]

This red sled
is fast as a jet,
the best yet on the hill!
I will bet that
I can sled
and never fall or spill.
This sled has sped
on all the hills.
It zips! It's fast! It's tops!
But do not tell
my mom or dad it
can
not
stop!

Text Analysis

Alphabetic Principle	Decoding/Encoding	Comprehension
• Phonemic Awareness: Phoneme segmentation of words with initial and final consonant blends (i.e., sled, sped, best, spill, stop).	• Use accurate sound-spelling associations	Ask literal and inferential questions

Activity Application to Text

Lesson development "Think Aloud"	Lesson Focus: Phonemic Awareness – Sound segmentation
	Activity: Say it and Move it (with tokens) (See page 28)
	Group Size: Small Group
This short decodable poem provides students with the opportunity to practice reading closed syllable words in context. The phoneme segmentation activity **Say it and Move it** can be used as a warm-up prior to reading the poem.	Materials needed: Say It and Move It boards; one for each student, tokens, list of two, three, four or five phoneme words (e.g., sled, sped, best, spill, stop), *This Red Sled* written on poster paper or a white board. How to do activity: 1. Teach or review the procedure for Say It and Move It (See page 28) 2. Explain that in preparation for reading the poem *The Red Sled*, they will practice taking several words apart, sound-by-sound. Each of these words comes from the poem and several of the words have a blend – most at the beginning but a few have a blend at the end. 3. Model the procedure with the word **sled**. Use the strategy of building from the "inside out" by segmenting with the word **led** first and then **sled**. Ask the students to try it. Provide corrective feedback where necessary. 4. Provide guided practice for each of the following words: **sled, sped, best, spill,** and **stop**. Use the "inside out" strategy to help students segment both sounds in the initial or final blend.

[2] "This Red Sled" © Karen G. Jordan 2007

Stage 1

Hickory Dickory Dock

Hickory Dickory dock,
The mouse ran up the clock,
The clock struck one
The mouse ran down,
Hickory Dickory dock.

Hickory Dickory dock,
The mouse ran up the clock,
The clock struck two
And down he flew,
Hickory Dickory dock.

Text Analysis

Alphabetic Principle	Decoding/Encoding	Comprehension
• Phonemic Awareness: Phoneme blending of individual sounds to make a word.	• Use accurate sound-spelling associations	Ask literal and inferential questions

Activity Application to Text

Lesson development "Think Aloud"	Lesson Focus: Phonemic Awareness – Sound blending
	Activity: Aliens from Outer Space (See page 32)
	Group Size: Small Group
The familiar poem *Hickory Dickory Dock* includes many one syllable words such as **clock**, **mouse**, and **up**. The activity **Aliens from Outer Space** provides practice blending individual sounds into whole words.	Materials needed: Picture of an alien or alien figure; list of two, three, four or five phoneme words (e.g., dock, mouse, up, clock, struck, down, two, and flew) How to do activity: 1. Tell students that friendly creatures called aliens from outer space came to earth. These creatures have a different way of talking. For example, for **cake** they say / k / / ā / / k /. For the word **dog** they say / d / / aw / / g /. 2. Tell students that you will say a word the way the aliens do, they have to say it the way humans (we) say it. 3. Explain that in preparation for reciting the poem *Hickory Dickory Dock*, you are going to talk like the aliens. When you do, you will use the following hand gesture: Start with your hands together in front of you and move them apart as you break apart the word into its component sounds. Demonstrate with the word dock: "The aliens say / d / / ŏ / / k /." 4. Tell students they will say the word the way we (humans) do. When you demonstrate saying the word, bring your hands together and clap. "We say / dock /." 5. Continue with additional words from the poem. Repeat hand gestures each time you deliver a word sound-by-sound and as you put the word back together.

Relevant Research in Phonics

What is it?

Phonics pertains to the knowledge of the association between sounds (phonemes) and letters (graphemes), what we refer to as alphabet knowledge. Phonics instruction requires teachers to understand the English language's writing system (orthography) – the rules that govern how sounds are mapped on to various spelling patterns. This knowledge gives students access to 85% of the words they need to read and spell.

While logical and rule-governed, English is not as transparent as some languages with one-to-one mapping systems (e.g., Spanish and Italian). In contrast, learning to read and spell in English requires understanding that there can be multiple ways to represent the same sound (e.g., $/\bar{a}/$ can be represented with **a_e**, **ai**, **ay**, **eigh** and so on). Phonics instruction should include teaching the skills of reading (decoding) and spelling (encoding) words reciprocally to reinforce students' understanding of their complementary relationship.

The ultimate goal of phonics instruction is to ensure that students can read each and every word accurately and automatically – that is, as a 'sight word.' Through explicit phonics instruction, beginning readers apply their alphabetic knowledge to read words by forming letter-sound (graphophonemic) connections so that words are secured in memory and read by sight. As part of this process, teachers must make sure that their students learn to distinguish between words that are phonetically regular (e.g., blast, stream, those, darling) and words that are phonetically irregular (e.g., *friend*, *through*, *their*, *said*). Understanding this distinction has instructional implications, which are discussed in the Knowledge for Effective Instruction and Activities for Instruction and Informal Assessment sections. Rather than spend students' precious instructional time memorizing arbitrary "sight word lists," students benefit from learning decoding procedures based on the alphabetic principle and practicing them while reading text with regular recognizable patterns (i.e., code-emphasis text) to build word reading fluency (i.e., accurate and automatic word recognition).

Let's take a look at what we know from research in relation to each stage.

	Developmental Sequence		
	Stage 0 (Grades Pre – K)	**Stage 1** (Grades K – 2)	**Stage 2** (Grades 2 – 3)
Focus of literacy development	Pre-alphabetic principle; letter naming	Alphabetic principle Decoding and encoding	Orthographic and morphologic patterns
What do we know from research?	• Among the reading readiness skills that are traditionally studied, letter naming appears to be the strongest predictor of later reading success (Snow, Burns, & Griffith, 1998). • "Writing serves as a type of laboratory, in which even very young children are actively creating and testing hypotheses about how writing works" (Cabell, Tortorelli, & Gerde, 2013). • "Allowing children to engage in the analytical process of invented spelling, followed by appropriate feedback, has been found to facilitate learning to read and spell, not hamper the process" (Ouellette & Senechal, 2016).	• Direct explicit instruction in sequential decoding develops the ability to attack unknown words. Beginning readers become more proficient in applying this strategy to decode unknown words and develop more sight words thus becoming more able to analyze words and become unglued from the print (Chall, 1967). • Teaching the vowel patterns ensures that about 85% of words can be decoded accurately (May, 1988). • Beginning readers learn to recognize words by sight by connecting the spelling of the word to its pronunciation – not by connecting the visual shape of the word to the word's meaning. (Ehri & McCormick, 1998) • The connection-forming process includes connecting the graphophonic information to meaning, which secures the 'sight word' in memory. There is convincing evidence that decoding skill plays an important role in reducing the number of exposures required for automatic identification of irregular words (Ehri, 2005; Share, 1995). • The correlation between spelling and reading	• As students advance, their ability to read will increase much more quickly than their ability to spell. Fluency (speed, accuracy, and expression) is one goal of instruction. Word knowledge will continue to improve as children engage in reading a variety of texts that expose them to many different words. "The trick is how to provide students with spelling instruction that promotes active, reflective thought about language that leads to improved reading, spelling, and writingl" (Carreker, Perspectives, 2005).

		Developmental Sequence	
		comprehension is high because both depend on a common denominator: proficiency with language. The more deeply and thoroughly a student knows a word, the more likely he or she is to recognize it, spell it, define it, and use it appropriately in speech and writing (Joshi et. al., 2009).	

English Learners
- Systematic phonics instruction can be very effective in helping ELs learn to decode words. The most effective reading programs for ELs combine systematic phonics instruction with a print-rich environment that provides exposure to appealing reading materials in varied genres (Irujo, 2007).

Students with dyslexia/reading disabilities
- In order to recognize words instantly, accurately and effortlessly, individuals must have good phonemic awareness, automatic letter-sound knowledge, and know how to blend the sounds accurately and automatically to read words. As dyslexic students begin to learn to read, they often have problems with word recognition because of difficulties with one, some or all of the aforementioned prerequisite skills (Seidenberg, 2017).
- Dyslexic students' reading fluency is often marked by inaccuracies and/or hesitancies when attempting to read the words. This error-prone reading often leads to dysfluent reading – another frequent characteristic of dyslexia (Kilpatrick, 2015).
- Results from a recent study indicated that integrating coding and decoding instruction in first-grade classrooms, as well as supplemental intervention programs, may be the missing links to decreasing and possibly preventing future reading problems for students previously at risk for reading disabilities (Weiser, 2012).
- Many children have specific word reading difficulties and as such, require explicit phonics instruction. "Individuals diagnosed with dyslexia may require more lengthy and intensive interventions—for example, with smaller teacher student ratios and more opportunities for practice—than do those who are curriculum casualties" (Spear-Swerling, 2015).
- Students with dyslexia whose phonological core deficit impacts decoding and encoding skills require explicit instruction in phonics. "In Typical Literacy Practice (TLP), beginning readers would usually read predictable or leveled texts that do not control for different phonics word patterns and therefore are challenging to decode" (Spear-Swerling, 2018).

KNOWLEDGE for Effective Instruction

Phonics, another one of the "ph" terms

Phonics is one of a trilogy of terms critical to know for teachers who provide literacy instruction. The three terms—phonological awareness, phonemic awareness, and phonics—are defined and illustrated in the following table.

Term	Definition	Examples
Phonological Awareness	Ability to identify and manipulate oral language at the level of word, rhyme or syllable	March to identify each word in a sentence Clap to identify each syllable in a word Categorize words beginning with the same sound Recognize if word pairs rhyme.
Phonemic Awareness	Ability to focus on and manipulate individual sounds (phonemes) in spoken words	Move a token to segment the sounds in **hat**. / h / / ă / / t / Blend these sounds / h / / ă / / t / = hat
Phonics	Ability to link spoken sounds to the letter or letter combinations that represent them	/ h / is represented by h / ch / is represented by ch or tch / ā / is represented by ai, ay, a_e, eigh

This book focuses on phonics, the ability to link spoken language sounds (phonemes) to the letter or letter combinations (graphemes) that represent them. The role of phonics instruction is to teach the letter or letter combinations that represent each sound.

The role of letter naming

While phonics focuses on linking sounds to letters, letter naming plays an important role, too. According to Adams (1990), "the single best predictor of first-year reading achievement is the child's knowledge of and the ability to recognize and name the upper- and lower-case letters of the alphabet." Why is letter naming important? First, letter names provide a common and consistent language to refer to the symbols of the alphabet. Letter names can also provide a bridge to learn the sound associated with the symbol. For example, the letter names for some letters are associated with their sound (e.g., **b** includes the sound / b /, **d** includes the sound / d /, and **z** includes the sound / z /). This phonemic overlap between the name and the sound of the letter facilitates learning both. Though this level of transparency between the letter name and the sound the letter represents doesn't happen for all letters, a study by Piasta and Wagner (2009) found that students who learned letter names in conjunction with letter sounds did better with letter-sound knowledge. Finally, in addition to letter naming being predictive of reading success, letter naming speed correlates with reading fluency (Neuhaus, 2003).

How should letter names be taught? Some differing points of view exists among researchers and educators in terms of what is meant by learning the letters of the alphabet. For some, it is limited to the name associated with the letter form. For others, this knowledge includes familiarity with all the properties of a letter, including its shape and sound, as well as its name. Letter names are important because they provide a category "label" for the various letter forms of the visual form (Seidenberg, 2017, p. 109). Some studies suggest that this more comprehensive knowledge of the letter increases the likelihood that the student will read it accurately and automatically (Ehri, 2005). Additionally, given the evidence of the positive impact of comprehensive letter knowledge on accurate and automatic word reading, it is advisable that instruction in all of the properties of the letters be concurrent rather than sequential. Regardless of how comprehensively properties of the letters are covered, instruction should include **all** the letters, including those used less frequently, and should ensure that every letter is recognized instantly.

The sounds behind the letters

Phonics is the dimension of literacy development through which students learn to represent the sounds (phonemes) with letters (graphemes). In English, there are 44 speech sounds organized into two categories—consonants and vowels. Understanding the distinction between these categories of sounds is foundational to effective phonics instruction.

Beyond the ability to manipulate phonemes in words (See pages 5 – 15 for more about phonemic awareness), the understanding that many of the phonemes can be represented in multiple ways is the bedrock for learning phonics. Knowing that there are limited and specific options for representing phonemes is a key concept for acquiring the alphabetic principle.

The sounds are categorized according to how they are produced. Consonant sounds restrict airflow during their production. Our speech organs - lips, teeth, or tongue – close off the flow of air. The following chart displays the 25 consonant sounds according to the position of the mouth, which indicates how air is restricted, and the type of consonant sound.

English Consonant Chart

Type of Consonant Sound	Bilabial (lips)	Labiodental (lips/teeth)	Dental (tongue between teeth)	Alveolar (tongue behind teeth)	Palatal (roof of mouth)	Velar (back of mouth)	Glottal (throat)
Stops	/p/ /b/			/t/ /d/		/k/ /g/	
Fricatives		/f/ /v/	/th/ /th/	/s/ /z/	/sh/ /zh/		/h/[1]
Affricatives					/ch/ /j/		
Nasals	/m/			/n/		/ng/	
Lateral				/l/			
Semivowels	/ʰw/ /w/[2]			/r/	/y/		

[1] Classed as a fricative on the basis of acoustic effect. It is like a vowel without voice.
[2] /ʰw/ and /w/ are velar as well as bilabial, as the back of the tongue is raised as it is for /u/.
Adapted with permission from Bolinger, D. 1975. *Aspects of Language* (2nd ed.). Harcourt Brace Jovanovich, p. 41.

*Some systems for counting the speech sounds yield 44 speech sounds.

A research project known as Project 1991 confirmed the consistency of phoneme-grapheme correspondences in English. This confirmation validated the idea of developing effective spelling programs based on the alphabetic principle (Hanna, Hodges & Hanna, 1971). In addition to this research that clarified the alphabetic nature of American-English spelling, findings from other studies examining instruction that emphasizes the reciprocal nature of spelling with decoding further supports a code-emphasis for literacy instruction ((Ehri, 2000; Ehri, 1997; Ehri, 1989). The Project 1991 findings also provided an important insight into the way a sound is represented in letters. Data showed that the way a sound is represented is predictable based on the of position of the sound in syllables or words. For example, the sound /f/ is represented with **ff** at the end of a single syllable word (e.g., **off**, **buff**) or the sound /k/ is encoded with **–ck** at the end of one-syllable words following a short vowel sound (e.g., **back**, **duck**). These patterns provide additional evidence of the regularity of the phoneme-grapheme correspondences, and thereby further inform the focus of phonics instruction.

With these concepts in mind, the consonant sounds in the English Consonant Chart above can be viewed in terms of their variant grapheme representations in the following table.

Sound-Symbol Correspondences for Consonant Sounds[1]

Phoneme	Grapheme	Examples	Phoneme	Grapheme	Examples	Phoneme	Grapheme	Examples
/ b /	b	bat, tab	/ m /	m, -mb[3], -mn[3]	mat, ham, bomb, hymn	/ w /	w	wet
/ k /	c, k, -ck[2]	cat, kit, back	/ n /	n, kn-[3]	nob, can, knit	/ ks /	x	six
/ d /	d	dog, mad	/ p /	p	pup	/ y /	y	yes
/ f /	f, ph, -ff[2]	fun, phone, off	/ kw /	qu	quit	/ z /	z, -zz[2]	zip, fuzz
/ g /	g	got, dig	/ r /	r, wr-[3]	rat, write	/ th /	th	that, smooth[4] thin, with
/ h /	h	hat	/ s /	s, c, -ss[2]	sun, cent, miss	/ ch /	ch, -tch[2]	chip, hatch
/ j /	j, g, -dge[2], -ge	jet, gist, hedge, cage	/ t /	t	ten, net	/ sh /	sh	ship, wish
/ l /	l, -ll[2]	lip, pill	/ v /	v	vet, rev	/ hw /	wh	when

[1] The focus of the grapheme representations in this table is on content typical for students in Stages 0 – 2 (i.e., the primary grades). More advanced representations such as / ch / represented by –ture, enter the scope and sequence of instruction
after the more transparent correspondences are mastered.
[2] The graphemes –ck, ff, ll, ss, zz, -dge and –tch are usually used to represent the designated phoneme in one-syllable words following a short vowel (e.g., **back**, **off**, **pill**, **miss**, **fuzz**, **hedge**, **hatch**)
[3] The non-bolded letter in these letter combinations are silent as in **bomb**, **knit**, and **write**.
[4] The grapheme **th** represents two sounds. The voiced **th** as in **that** and smooth or the voiceless **th** as in **thin** and **with**.

In contrast, vowel sounds do not restrict the flow of air during their production. They are referred to as open sounds. Vowels are the language sounds that form the nucleus of a syllable. A vowel sound—with or without consonants—forms whole or parts of words. For example, a single vowel sound can be a word such as "I" or "a." A single vowel can also be a syllable in a multi-syllable word, such as the i in item. The number of syllables in a word is equal to the number of vowel sounds (e.g., one syllable in tree; two syllables in meatball; three syllables in volcano). See the section "Units of decodabiity" page 48 for more about syllables.

Vowel sounds are produced by subtle changes in the position and height of the tongue. The following table maps out the vowel sounds. Most vowel sounds are represented by multiple graphemes. The list of words below each of the vowel sounds in the table (e.g., long **o** has five grapheme representations: **o**, **o_e**, **oa**, **ow**, and **oe**) are listed in order of frequency of use, an important concept to convey through instruction. For example, when spelling long **o**, the graphemic pattern **o_e** (e.g., in words like **bone**, **tote**, **rose**) is used more often than **oa** (e.g., in words like **boat**, **toast**, **roam**). This knowledge—in conjunction

with repeated exposures to words using each grapheme representation—is helpful to students in terms of both reading (decoding) and spelling (encoding) words.

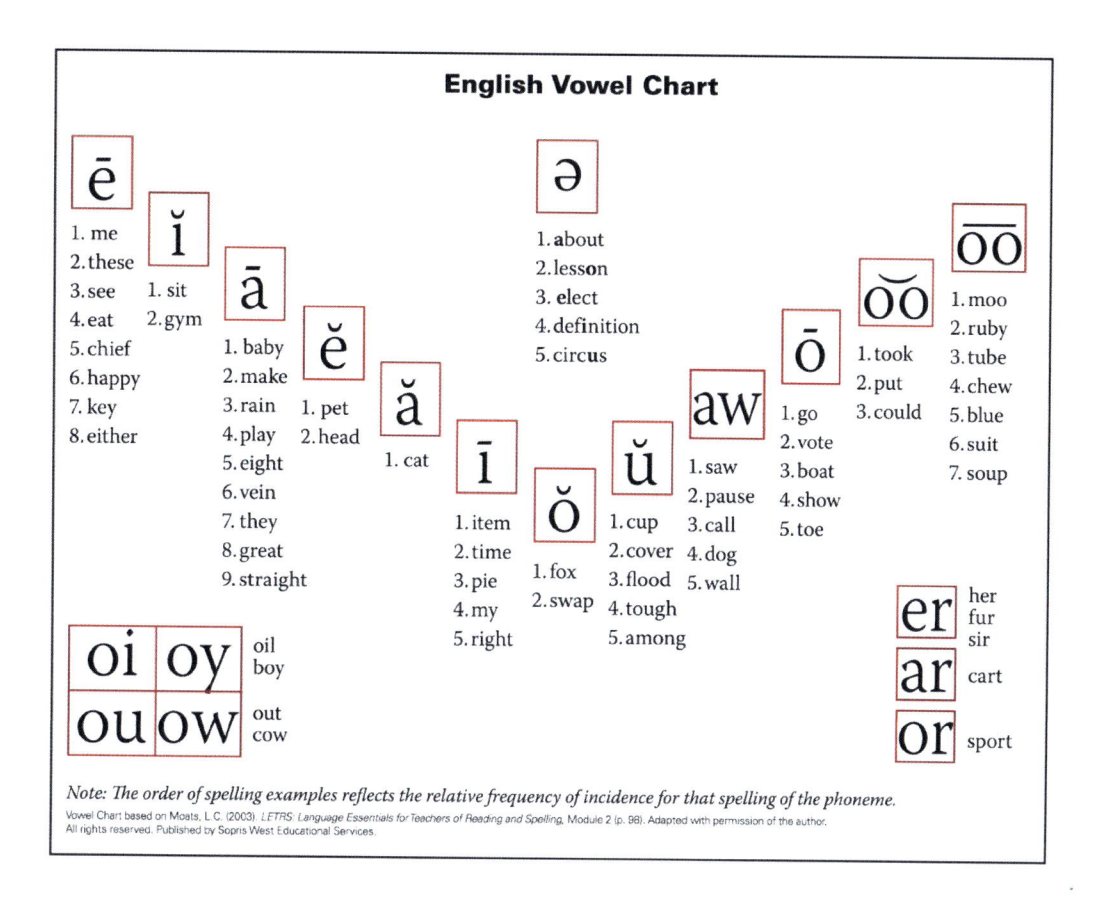

English Vowel Chart

ē	1. me 2. these 3. see 4. eat 5. chief 6. happy 7. key 8. either
ĭ	1. sit 2. gym
ā	1. baby 2. make 3. rain 4. play 5. eight 6. vein 7. they 8. great 9. straight
ĕ	1. pet 2. head
ă	1. cat
ī	1. item 2. time 3. pie 4. my 5. right
ŏ	1. fox 2. swap
ŭ	1. cup 2. cover 3. flood 4. tough 5. among
ə	1. about 2. lesson 3. elect 4. definition 5. circus
aw	1. saw 2. pause 3. call 4. dog 5. wall
ō	1. go 2. vote 3. boat 4. show 5. toe
o͝o	1. took 2. put 3. could
o͞o	1. moo 2. ruby 3. tube 4. chew 5. blue 6. suit 7. soup
oi / oy	oil / boy
ou / ow	out / cow
er	her, fur, sir
ar	cart
or	sport

Note: The order of spelling examples reflects the relative frequency of incidence for that spelling of the phoneme.
Vowel Chart based on Moats, L. C. (2003). *LETRS: Language Essentials for Teachers of Reading and Spelling*, Module 2 (p. 98). Adapted with permission of the author. All rights reserved. Published by Sopris West Educational Services.

For instructional guidance regarding sound production, see the **Mirror Mouth** activity on page 21.

In the case of both consonants and vowels, we see that there is often not a one-to-one correspondence between the sounds (phonemes) and the letters (graphemes) used to represent them. Unlike languages with a shallow orthography (e.g., Spanish), in which a nearly one-to-one relationship exists between sound-spelling correspondences, English is a language with a deep orthography – that is, it has multiple spellings for many of its speech sounds. Furthermore, there are frequent instances in English when words sound the same but are spelled differently with unique meanings associated with each spelling. For example, the word pronounced /per/ in English can be spelled **pair** (i.e., two of the same thing), **pear** (i.e., a juicy fruit), or **pare** (i.e., to cut back). In contrast, each of these meanings in Spanish has a uniquely different word associated with it (e.g., **par** meaning two of the same thing; **pera** meaning a juicy fruit; **cortar** meaning to cut back). These factors—multiple spellings for the same sound and differing meanings for words that sound the same—make English more difficult to learn than a language with a shallow orthography. English's deep orthography necessitates systematic, cumulative and explicit instruction of phonics skills, as well as careful attention to the meanings associated with the spelling of similar-sounding words. While phonemic awareness lays the foundation for students to associate the sounds with their written symbols, the deep orthographic characteristics of English requires a carefully articulated presentation of encoding and meaning options to facilitate learning to the point of mastery. (See the "Advanced phonics" section for more about this morphophonemic aspect of English on page 49.)

Units of decodability

The emphasis in phonics instruction is initially on phoneme-grapheme correspondences to read words (i.e., to go from print to speech) or to spell words (i.e., go from speech to print). At this phase of instruction, the unit of decodability is the one-to-one correspondence of the sounds (phonemes) in the word to the graphemes that represent them. The following table shows this relationship.

Word	Phonemes	Graphemes
hat	/h/ / ă / / t /	h – a – t
hatch	/h/ / ă / / ch /	h – a – tch
thatch	/th/ / ă / / ch /	th – a – tch

Phoneme-grapheme associations are the building blocks of syllables, the next larger unit of decodability. Most words in English are composed of a single or a combination of six syllable types. Syllable types are identified by the position of the vowel (V); the position of the vowel signals how the vowel sound is pronounced. For example, when the vowel is followed by one or more consonants (i.e., closed in), the vowel sound is typically short (e.g., **bat, batch**). In contrast, when a vowel ends a syllable (i.e., not followed by a consonant so the syllable is open), the vowel sound is usually long (e.g., **be**). The following table presents the six syllable types, their patterns and vowel sounds. Teaching students to recognize the position of vowels within syllable provides them with a strategy to determine the pronunciation of unfamiliar letter combinations (See **Syllable Inspectors** page 84) and an essential understanding to divide longer words into pronounceable units.

Syllable type	Pattern	Vowel sound	Examples
Closed	VC, CVC	Short vowel	at, Ed, it, on, up; cap, bit, pet, tot, cut
Open	CV	Long vowel	be, I, my
Silent e	VCe	Long vowel	cape, bite, Pete, tote, cute

Syllable type	Pattern	Vowel sound	Examples
Vowel teams[1] • Talker pattern • Whiner pattern	VV	Long vowel Vowel sound is neither long nor short but a different sound called a diphthong	rain, boat, free boil, boy; out, down
R-controlled	Vr	Vowel sound is neither long nor short but is influenced by **r** that follows the vowel letter	far, for, her, fir, fur
Consonant-le	C-le	Vowel sound is schwa	can*dle*, ta*ble*, gur*gle*

[1]Cheyney, W.S. and Cohen, E.J. (1999). *Focus on phonics: Assessment and instruction.* Bothell, WA: The Wright Group/McGraw-Hill, pp. 32 – 33.

While phoneme-grapheme knowledge and syllable types make up the major content for decoding words, morphology (i.e., meaningful parts) can also provide insight to read and spell words – especially those words that have prefixes, suffixes, or both. The way that morphology contributes to decoding and encoding words is addressed in the vocabulary domain, along with morphology's role in unlocking word meaning (See *Vocabulary: Knowledge to Practice* in the Literacy How Professional Learning Series.)

Advanced phonics

Phonics instruction isn't finished when students master the consonant sounds, short vowel sounds, and closed syllables. These basic concepts are the foundation from which additional sounds, letter combinations, and syllable patterns develop. When teachers explicitly teach advanced phonics skills, it enables their students to read and spell a wider range of words, including those composed of more than one syllable. As students make progress in learning more complex phonics skills, they learn about the intersection of the units of decodability—letters, syllables and morphemes—and meaning (i.e., English is a morphophonemic language).

One important insight that students need to acquire is that merely pronouncing a word doesn't guarantee knowing the word's meaning. Homophones, words that have the same pronunciation but different meanings and spellings, provide a good example of the importance of this concept. The following words— **sent**, **cent** and **scent**—are pronounced the same way (i.e., / s ĕ n t /, however, the meaning of each word is different (i.e., **sent** is the past of the verb to send; **cent** is one hundredth of a dollar; **scent** refers to a distinction smell, such as of a flower). While sound-symbol knowledge can help readers go from the printed word to its spoken equivalent, the context of a phrase or sentence is required to learn the correct meaning to associate with each spelling of the same-sounding word.

Advanced phonics also emphasizes strategies to read multi-syllable words. In addition to learning the characteristics of the six syllable types (See "Units of decodability" page 48), instruction must emphasize the patterns that facilitate syllable division. The goal of syllable division is to break long words into pronounceable parts. This process is driven by the number of vowels in the word; every vowel sound is the basis for a syllable. The basic syllable division patterns are:

Syllable division pattern	Sample Word	Syllable division and pronunciation
VC/CV	napkin	n ă p/k ĭ n
V/CV	pilot	p ī /l o t[1]
VC/V	lemon	l ĕ m/o n[1]
V/V	lion	l ī/o n[1]
VC/CCV	hundred	h ŭ n /d r ĕ d

[1]The vowels in the second syllable of these words are not marked short or long. In an unaccented syllable, the vowel sound is reduced to schwa. See *Schwa*llowed **Vowels** activity page 69 for more about the schwa sound.

Determining the position of the vowel in the syllable signals how to pronounce the vowel. For example, the vowel **a** in **nap** is short because the vowel is followed by a consonant (**p**), which makes it a closed syllable with a short vowel sound. In contrast, the vowel **i** in **pi** is long because the vowel ends the syllable, which make it an open syllable with a long vowel sound.

Another approach to dividing words into smaller chunks involves identifying morpheme units (i.e., prefixes, roots, and suffixes). As students acquire sight recognition of prefixes and suffixes, these units of meaning contribute to an efficient approach to decoding multi-syllable words (e.g., **previewing** = **pre** + **view** + **ing**). Using the affixes (e.g., **pre-**, **-ing**) as part of the strategy to read **previewing**, simplifies the process. In this case, after identifying the prefix and suffix parts, the reader is left to decode only the base of the word, **view**. The use of affixes to "attack" words has an additional advantage, namely that morphemes provide both a phonemic and semantic (i.e., meaning) layer to decoding the word (e.g., **previewing** means looking at something before).

Not all words are phonetically predictable

While approximately 85 percent of words in English are decodable based on their phonemic and syllabic regularities, that does leave a small percent of words that do not follow the phoneme-grapheme correspondences that yields the correct pronunciation of these words. Additionally, some of these irregular words, often of Anglo-Saxon origin, are among the first 100 high frequency words found in print.

(See Appendix page 145 for the list of the first 100 high frequency words.) For example, the word **the** is the number one most frequently used word in English but is not pronounced with a long **e** sound for the vowel as is true with other open syllable words ending in **e** (e.g., **be, me, we**). Since a number of these "rule-breaking" words are among the most frequently used words in English, it is important for students to learn to recognize these words accurately and automatically.

Orthographic mapping

Automatic word recognition is essential to be a fluent reader. This means a reader must recall words effortlessly and instantly. Words that are recognized and recalled this way are referred to as sight words. This term—sight words—applies to words that are phonetically regular (e.g., **top, bone**), as well as those that are not phonetically regular (e.g., **was, said**).

How do words become sight words? Several decades ago, Adams explained that "it is automatic, frequency-based pattern recognition that is responsible for the speed and reliability with which skillful readers process the spellings, sounds and meanings of words and the spellings and sounds of pseudowords." (Adams, 1990, p. 211) More recently, Kilpatrick described this concept as orthographic mapping, which he defines as "the process that readers use to store written words for instant and effortless retrieval. It is the means by which readers turn unfamiliar written words into familiar and instantly recognizable sight words (Kilpatrick, 2015)."

Novice readers need to learn when to apply their sound-symbol knowledge to decode words (See the **Build and Blend** activity on page 80) and how to recognize phonetically irregular words through other strategies (See the **Rule Breakers… Beware!** activity on page 104). With practice in code-emphasis text, decodable words become sight words. As the pool of sight words grows, students need less controlled text and will add more and more phonetically irregular words to their sight word vocabulary.

How do students advance from learning words one-by-one to more rapid word acquisition? Several instructional practices can contribute to students' progress in orthographic mapping. One practice focuses on advanced phonemic awareness skills. These include phoneme substitution (e.g., Change the / l / in **slow** to / t /… **stow**), deletion (e.g., Say **stow** without the / s / … **tow**), and reversal (e.g., Say **pitch**. Now say the sounds in reverse…**chip**). The ability to perform these advanced phonemic manipulation tasks automatically appears to be needed for efficient sight vocabulary development (Kilpatrick, 2015). Another instructional practice contributing to orthographic mapping involves abundant practice with letter patterns in print to help readers move beyond letter-by-letter analysis. With repeated encounters with letter patterns, such as common rime units (e.g., **-at, -old, -et**), readers begin to detect letter patterns—

words or word parts—through practice and redundancies in print. As smaller words or syllables are recognized instantly, that knowledge transfers to unfamiliar words with the same patterns to facilitate recognizing them instantly. This process of unitizing letter sequences (i.e., the sequence becomes a recognized unit) accelerates the overall development of word recognition (Murry, 2018). For example, the reader, who has learned to recognize the word **let** (i.e., / l ĕ t /) through practice reading word lists and code-emphasis text containing numerous words with short vowel **e** (i.e., / ĕ /) will begin to recognize that letter pattern in unfamiliar words such as **let**tuce, ham**let**, and book**let**, which facilitates reading the new words. (See "The text we choose to use" section on page 53 for more on the role of code-emphasis text.)

Features of effective instructional practices

Researchers have identified effective practices to teach literacy concepts and skills. Let's see how these practices apply to phonics instruction.

- **Explicit instruction**: Explicit instruction means direct teaching of content, strategies and skills. In the case of phonics, explicit instruction focuses on the alphabetic principle, which is the term used for the relationship between the sounds of spoken language (phonemes) and the letters of written language (graphemes). The use of code-emphasis text, which allows for direct application of the content learned in phonics lessons to read text, is another example of explicit instruction (See "The text we choose to use" and "The importance of code-emphasis (aka decodable) text" sections on pages 53 through 57 for more information about code-emphasis text.)

- **Emphasis on making abstract concepts concrete**: Multisensory techniques—including tangible objects, visuals, graphics and color coding and kinesthetic techniques—help to make abstract concepts concrete. For example, individual letter cards can be used to make the task of word building concrete (See the activity **Build and Blend** page 80). Sound letter maps concretely show the encoding process (See the activity **Sound-Letter Maps** page 69). Both techniques make abstract language elements manipulative.

- **Emphasis on automaticity**: Automaticity helps overcome a key obstacle to learning—the limited capacity of working memory. A main goal of phonics is for students to blend the sounds represented by graphemes automatically into words. Guidelines for targeted correct words per minute (CWPM) make it possible to gauge that students are on a trajectory for fluent reading (See the activity **Beat the Clock** page 110). Reading code-emphasis text (i.e., decodable text) also contributes to developing accuracy and automaticity, because it facilitates readers' ability to attend to and use their code knowledge. The controlled nature and decodability of this type of text ensures that the reader's efforts will be successful. The development of sight word recognition, that is the ability to recognize a word without going through the process of sounding out, is another dimension of automaticity that ultimately contributes to greater attention to text comprehension.

- **Development of meta-cognitive strategies**: Meta-cognitive strategies focus on the awareness or analysis of what one is learning. Strategies, such as chunking words into syllable units, teach students to attend to the syllable structure of words and to use that knowledge to systematically analyze long words into pronounceable parts. Another important meta-cognitive strategy is grouping words into meaningful phrases or grammatical entities to help students develop reading fluency and to facilitate comprehension. (For more information about grammar and phrases see *Syntax: Knowledge to Practice* in the Literacy How Professional Learning Series.)

- **Stress on cumulative, systematic, and sequential presentation of content and skills**: The foundation of English—such as its sound-spelling correspondences and syllable patterns—should be presented in a logical order. This order is typically represented by a scope and sequence outlined in a curriculum or program. Scope and sequences may vary. Regardless of the variations, adhering to the scope and sequence to the point of mastery is critically important to develop accurate and automatic decoding and encoding.

- **Use of data to guide instruction**: Evidence of learning—be it mastery of sound-spelling correspondences or CWPM—provides critical data to inform the focus and pacing of instruction. Additionally, performance data from screening tools (e.g., DIBELS, AIMSweb, easyCBM) indicate whether or not students are on the necessary trajectory to be skilled decoders by third grade. (See Appendix page 148 for word reading fluency norms.)

The text we choose to use

As part of phonics instruction, attention to the type of text we use is essential to maximize that instruction. Not all text provides optimal characteristics to master the application of phoneme-grapheme knowledge. Let's take a look at the different types of text to see how each type plays a specific role in the early stages of learning to read.

The types of text we use with students evolve across the stages of reading development and reflect the oral language of students and the level of their facility in using the code to figure out words (i.e., "learn to read"), and the eventual shift to "read to learn." Accordingly, we can label the types of text by these stages of reading development as follows:

- **Stage 0: Predictable Text** – The language in this type of text is based on oral language patterns and structures. These texts are characterized by repeated words and phrases that children can remember and repeat. At this stage, children give the impression of reading the words, when in fact they are often mimicking what has been read to them.

- **Stage 1: Code-emphasis Text** – This type of text, also referred to as decodable, is designed to practice beginning decoding skills and a small number of sight words. The goal is to have abundant encounters with sound-spelling patterns (i.e., the code) that students have learned in order to become automatic in accurately recognizing and reading the words. This text frequently sounds less like talking because the word selection is more controlled according to specific decoding skills.
- **Stage 2: Authentic** – At this stage, text selections provide opportunities to develop fluency with self-confirmation of accuracy and ease of understanding.

Let's examine each type of text in terms of its characteristic, purpose, and impact on becoming a proficient reader.

	Stage 0 Predictable	Stage 1 Code-emphasis	Stage 2 Authentic
Characteristics	<ul><li>Syntactic repetition</li><li>Use of concrete pictures that reflect meaning</li><li>Rely on use of syntactic and semantic cues (i.e., patterns familiar from spoken language)</li></ul>	<ul><li>High proportion of words with phonically regular relationships between letters and sounds</li><li>High degree of match between the letter/sound relationships represented in text and those that the reader has been taught (i.e., phonics instruction)</li><li>Value of code-emphasis text is contingent upon the degree to which the phonics lessons and the code-emphasis text are aligned</li></ul>	<ul><li>Word selection based on the content of the story or information rather than specific syntactic or phonetic features</li></ul>

	Stage 0 Predictable	Stage 1 Code-emphasis	Stage 2 Authentic
Purpose	• Bridges the transition from spoken to written language • Supports learning concepts of print	• Helps readers transition from a pre- and partial alphabetic stage to a more balanced word identification approach, including alphabetic knowledge • Supports the readers' efforts at word identification • Provides for application of letter/sound knowledge that students have learned to connected text. • Directs the reader's attention to letters and sounds	• Provides text to apply word identification skills to increase accuracy and automaticity • Uses more varied and complex sentence structure to facilitate the development of prosody (i.e., reading with phrasing based on meaning-based units)

	Stage 0 Predictable	Stage 1 Code-emphasis	Stage 2 Authentic
Sample text	The following excerpt from a familiar children's book illustrates features of predictable text. This text utilizes repetition of words and phrases, which are supported explicitly with illustrations. The structure of each stanza repeats with the substitution of new animals making it easier for children to "read" the text. *Brown Bear*[1] By Bill Martin & Eric Carle "Brown Bear, Brown Bear, What do you see?" "I see redbird looking at me."	The following sentence illustrates highly controlled code-emphasis text. 　My hat is big and red. This text uses a combination of - High frequency words (**my** and **is**) usually memorized in early grades because they use less-common letter-sound associations (e.g., **y** representing long **i**) - Words composed of letters representing their most frequently used sounds (e.g., consonants h, t, b, g, r, and d; short vowel sounds for a and i); letter-sound associations that students would have learned by the time they attempted to read the sentence. The decodability of this sample sentence is predicated on the phonetic regularity of the words and the match to previous phonics instruction.[2]	The following excerpt from the Common Core State Standards, Appendix B Text Exemplars illustrates authentic text. *Where Do Polar Bears Live?*[3] By Sarah Thomson "When the cub was born four months ago, he was no bigger than a guinea pig. Blind and helpless, he snuggled in his mother's fur. He drank her milk and grew, safe from the long Arctic winter." This text uses a combination of - High frequency words (e.g., **was**, **the**, **from**) - Low frequency, content-specific words (e.g., **guinea pig**) - Words composed of a more extensive level of phonic elements (e.g., final consonant blends such as **-nk** as in **drank**; lower-frequency vowel patterns such as **ew** as in **grew**) - Words with morphological elements (e.g., **-er** in **bigger**; **-less** in **helpless**) - More syntactically complex sentences requiring parsing (i.e., phrasing) of words into meaningful phrases and clauses - Pronoun referents (e.g., **he** for **cub**; **her** for **mother**) to promote text cohesion

[1] Martin, B. & Carle, E. (1967)
[2] Cheatham and Allor (2012)
[3] Thomson, Sarah L. (2010)

The importance of code-emphasis (aka decodable) text

Code-emphasis text, constructed from the sound-letter correspondences that are explicitly taught in phonics instruction, provides students with practice applying these skills. This type of text makes it possible for students to rely on the use of their phonics knowledge to decode words rather than resort to guessing. Skilled readers attend to each letter in a word and in fact "identify words quickly with little help from context" (Rayner et. al, 2001). Code-emphasis text allows beginning readers to acquire this all-important skill. Additionally, the use of decodable text allows teachers to focus explicitly on the decoding process in the model of reading referred to as The Simple View of Reading (SVR). This widely-accepted model makes clear the distinction and separate contribution of decoding (D) and language comprehension (LC) to reading comprehension (RC), emphasizing the role that each component plays in learning to read and comprehend text. Each component in the SVR requires explicit and differing instructional emphasis. When teachers are focused on teaching decoding, the text they use should support students' word recognition skills through the use of code-emphasis text.

Clearly any given text selection can span the characteristics and purposes of several stages, however choosing text should be influenced by the instructional purpose, or as Adams suggests, the feature of reading we want students to attend to. Adams points out that, "The supportive features in any text, be they repeated words, supportive pictures, rhyming words, or consistency between letters and sounds, affect that to which beginning readers attend (Adams, 1997)." For example, readers who apply letters and sounds during connected reading must be attending consciously to them; decodable text encourages this attention (Mesmer, 2005). For this reason, awareness of and ability to identify different types of text selections are fundamental to the instructional planning process.

A word about leveled readers

Leveled readers, the type of text used in guided reading and many core reading programs, can contribute to a practice in which teachers skip an integral stage of reading development – that is, Stage 1, the Alphabetic Stage. (See Chall's Stages of Reading Development chart on page 2.) The pervasive use of the three cueing systems with leveled readers shortchanges students by not providing them an opportunity to focus on the essential skill of learning the alphabetic principle to break the code. More akin to authentic text, leveled readers presume that students have mastered decoding and encoding skills (i.e., phonics) without providing code-emphasis, or decodable, text that supports applying this knowledge. Teachers are encouraged to use the type of text appropriate to the skills students are attempting to develop. This would suggest that leveled readers be used in Stage 2 and beyond as a type of authentic text, *after* students have learned the code.

Cognitive preparation for text utilization as part of phonics instruction

Text utilization is a key component of effective phonics instruction. In fact, teachers' cognitive preparation for phonics instruction should include a conscious and deliberate selection of code-emphasis text that is in alignment with the scope and sequence of phoneme-grapheme instruction. Text designed to practice the phoneme-grapheme associations that students have learned should include at least 80 percent of the words using those associations that have been taught. For example, the following poem *This Red Sled* by Karen Jordan would be a workable text selection after students have learned all of the short sounds for vowels. While there are some words which do not have a short vowel sound (e.g., **the**, **all**, **fall**, **I**), more than 80 percent of the words do (e.g., **fast**, **sled**, **will**, **not**, **but**). This high percentage of words adhering to the phonics knowledge that the students have acquired makes it possible for them to focus on using that knowledge with a high degree of assurance that they can sound out the words correctly.

> This red sled
> is fast as a jet,
> the best yet on the hill!
> I will bet that
> I can sled
> and never fall or spill.
> This sled has sped
> on all the hills.
> It zips! It's fast! It's tops!
> But do not tell
> my mom or dad it
> can
> not
> stop!

While students are learning the letter-sound associations, they need abundant practice applying their knowledge to text. The goal is to develop accurate and automatic decoding in context. Often this text is less conducive to an emphasis on "deep" comprehension, though it remains important to check for understanding even with code-emphasis text. (See *Comprehension: Knowledge to Practice* in the Literacy How Professional Development Series (in press) for more on comprehension instruction suited to each text type.)

Activities for Instruction and Informal Assessment

The activities in this section are designed to ensure that students can decode the vast majority of words for which letter-sound knowledge leads to accurate pronunciation—that is going from print to speech. To do this, the activities develop students' ability to associate sounds (phonemes) with the letter or letter combinations (graphemes) that represent them, an ability necessary to read (decode) and spell (encode) words. Instruction in this domain progresses from teaching transparent correspondences first (i.e., those with a one-to-one correspondence, such as **m** for / m /; **a** for / ă /) to those that are represented by letter combinations (e.g., **sh** for / sh /; **ai** for / ā /. The progression also includes sounds that can be spelled with multiple letter combinations (e.g., / ā / can be represented by **ai**, **ay**, or **a _ e** where the underscore is a consonant). See Appendix pages 93 through 99 for examples of this progression. In addition to the phoneme/grapheme associations, six syllable types—based on vowel patterns—provide the basis for decoding multi-syllable words.

While most of the activities in the phonics domain focus on phonetically regular words, instruction must also ensure that students learn to recognize and read phonetically irregular words. To accomplish this, specific activities help students learn the parts of the words that do not follow the sound-letter correspondences and provide practice with this group of words until they are recognized on sight (i.e., automatically and accurately).

These activities in the phonics domain involve:
- Concepts of print—track words in print by applying the alphabetic principle
- Phoneme/grapheme acquisition—associate the letter or letter combinations (graphemes) that represent speech sounds (phonemes) (e.g., **b** represents / b /; **ch** represents / ch /)
- Reading and spelling words—break a word into its sounds (phonemes) or syllable parts to facilitate spelling (encoding); combine the sounds (phonemes) for a sequence of letters (graphemes) to read a word (decoding)
- Syllable pattern identification—use vowel pattern recognition to classify and read six types of syllables
- Phonetically irregular words—identify and read words in which some part of the relationship between their pronunciation and spelling don't match (e.g., said - / s ĕ d /)
- Automatic word recognition—develop accurate and rapid reading of words (phonetically regular and irregular) as "sight words"

The activities in this domain include:

	Stage 0	Stage 1	Stage 2
Instruction	\multicolumn{3}{l|}{**Concepts of Print (See page 62)**}		
	Synchronized Reading (Track print using alphabetic principle)		
	\multicolumn{3}{l|}{**Phoneme-Grapheme Acquisition (See page 64)**}		
	Alphabet Chant (Associate letter name with letter symbols) Vowel Song (Learn most common sounds for each vowel) See It…Say It…Write It (Associate letters with sound and written representation)	Sound-Letter Maps (Map phonemes to graphemes)	Sound-Letter Maps (Map phonemes to graphemes)
	\multicolumn{3}{l|}{**Reading and Spelling Words (See page 72)**}		
	Invented Writing (Apply alphabetic principle to write words)	Listen and Write (Use letter-sound knowledge to write words) Build and Blend (Combine sounds to make words)	Listen and Write (Use letter-sound knowledge to write words) Build and Blend (Combine sounds to make words)
	\multicolumn{3}{l|}{**Syllable Pattern Identification (See page 82)**}		
		Syllable Inspectors (Identify syllable types) Syllable Sort (Categorize syllable based on type)	Syllable Inspectors (Identify syllable types) Syllable Sort (Categorize syllable based on type) *Schwa*llowed Vowels (Learn the schwa sound)
	\multicolumn{3}{l|}{**Phonetically Irregular Words (See page 103)**}		
		Rule Breakers…Beware! (Read irregular words)	Rule Breakers… Beware! (Read irregular words)
	\multicolumn{3}{l|}{**Automatic Word Recognition (See page 107)**}		
		Fluent Reading (Read words in phrases with prosody) Beat the Clock (Read words and phrases accurately and automatically)	Fluent Reading (Read words in phrases with prosody) Beat the Clock (Read words and phrases accurately and automatically)

	Stage 0	Stage 1	Stage 2
Informal Assessment	The following links are suggested as the kinds of assessments that are available to evaluate children's phonics skills. They are provided as examples and are not intended to be exhaustive. Readers are also encouraged to explore the assessments included as part of published programs that they use or through local and state assessment systems. CORE Phonics Survey (Scholastic Red) http://www.scholastic.com/dodea/module_2/resources/dodea_m2_tr_core.pdf San Diego Quick Assessment http://www.voyagersopris.com/rewardsintermediateresources/assets/testingdirectionsandmaterials_sdq.pdf		

Concepts of Print

The following activity focuses on tracking words in text using knowledge of the alphabetic principle.

Domain: Phonics

Background information for this activity:

Learning the alphabetic principle—that is that speech maps onto print, that words are discrete units with boundaries (i.e., beginning and final sounds), and that words are separated by spaces—requires guidance and practice. Knowledge of these concepts are part of the transition from understanding and using oral language to understanding written language (i.e., print). Through repeated readings of text with simple and repetitive sentence structure, students can focus on the relationship between the word units and the letter-sound associations within those words.

Stage 0	Stage 1	Stage 2
Synchronized Reading • Track print using knowledge of the alphabetic principle		

Concepts of Print: Synchronized Reading (Stage 0)

Objective: To practice finger point reading to develop awareness of the alphabetic principle

Target students: Pre-K – K

Materials needed: Short text (i.e., nursery rhymes, poems) written on poster paper or displayed on Smartboard, a pointer, and copies of the text for students' use

How to do activity:
1. Project or post the text for all students to see.
2. On the first reading, ask students to listen to the poem as you recite it slowly and with prosody. Point to each word as you read. Emphasize the following in one of the recitations:
    - Reading from the top of the page to the bottom
    - Reading words from left to right
    - Return sweep at the end of each row.
    - Some words get two taps because they have two parts (i.e., syllables)
3. During the second reading of the poem, stop intermittently to explain that the word you are pointing to begins with a sound that corresponds to/matches the letter (e.g., the word **soup** begins with the / s / sound and it has the letter **s** at the beginning of the word). Teach the same concept with an ending continuant sound (e.g., the word **muffin** ends with the / n / sound and it has the letter **n** at the end of the word). Encourage students to pay attention to what their mouths are saying along with the letters they are seeing. Synchronizing their attention between the sounds and letters helps students develop the alphabetic principle.
4. Provide students with a copy of the text at their seat/table. Recite the poem several more times and ask students to point to the words on their copy as you read.
5. Finally, ask individual children to 'read' the poem in front of the class with the pointer. Guide each child through the process, pointing out the match between what their mouth is saying and the sounds that the letter they are pointing to represents.

Follow-up Activity:

Write each line of the poem on a sentence strip. As an independent activity (i.e., a center activity), ask pairs of students to arrange the sentence strips in the correct order on a pocket chart.

Phoneme-Grapheme Acquisition

The following activities focus on establishing knowledge of the phoneme-to-grapheme associations needed to read and spelling words in English.

Domain: Phonics

Background information for this activity:

The ability to accurately name the letters of the alphabet is an important precursor to developing the alphabetic principle. Letter name knowledge is particularly critical to the spelling (encoding) process in which the distinction between the phonemes and the graphemes that represent them depends on knowing the letter names (See **Alphabet Chant** activity page 66). Additionally, letter naming is one of the best longitudinal predictors of learning to read (Snow, Burns & Griffith, 1998), thus warranting explicit instructional attention and ongoing monitoring.

Learning the vowel sounds is one of the most difficult aspects of the code. The multiple sounds for each vowel and multiple ways to encode them is what makes the vowel component challenging. Before students focus on the multiple spellings of the vowels, it is helpful for them to be able to discriminate between the two most common sounds for each vowel—short and long (See **Vowel Song** activity page 67). The ability to accurately distinguish short from long vowel sounds lays an important foundation to learn their grapheme representations.

The foundation of learning to read and spell is mastery of the sound-letter associations of the language. It is essential that students develop an automatic association linking the sounds (auditory), letters (visual) and written formation (kinesthetic/tactile) features of each letter of the alphabet (See **See It…Say It…Write It** page 68). These associations need to be taught explicitly and cumulatively following a scope and sequence[1] to ensure that students can automatically link each letter with its sound and written formation.

To master the alphabetic principle, students must identify the number of sounds (phonemes) in a word[2] and then associate the letter or letters (graphemes) that represent each sound. Mapping the graphemes to the phonemes moves students from phonemic awareness to phonics (See **Sound-Letter Maps** page 67). The acquisition of this knowledge—namely the predictable relationship between spoken sounds and the written letters that represent them—is at the heart of mastering the code to read and spell.

Stage 0	Stage 1	Stage 2
Alphabet Chant (Learn letter names using song for repetition) Vowel Song (Use song format to learn the most common sounds (short and long) for each vowel) See It…Say It…Write It (Learn association of letters with sounds and their written representation)	Sound-Letter Maps (Associate phonemes to graphemes using maps)	Sound-Letter Maps (Associate phonemes to graphemes using maps)

[1] Appendix page 127 provides a suggested scope and sequence to teach letter-sound associations. If teachers use a program that provides a scope and sequence, they are encouraged to use it for consistency within the program.

[2] This activity builds upon **Say It and Move It** in the Activities for Instruction and Informal Assessment section in *Phonemic Awareness: Knowledge to Practice* in the Literacy How Professional Development Series.

Phoneme-Grapheme Acquisition: Alphabet Chant (Stage 0)

Objective: To recite the alphabet synchronizing the name with the letter symbols

Target students: Pre-K – K

Materials needed: The Alphabet Chant chart—upper and lower case letterforms[1]

How to do activity:

1. Display the Alphabet Chant chart for upper case letterforms.[2]

The Alphabet Chant

A B C D E F G 👏
H I J K L M N 👏
O P Q 👏
R S T 👏
U V W 👏
X Y Z 👏

2. While pointing to each letter, model how to say the name[3] for the letter, pausing to clap as designated on the chart.
3. Have students repeat along with you as you name the letters. Be sure to synchronize saying the name for the letter to which you are pointing.
4. Invite individual students to name the letters as you point.
5. Repeat this activity daily allowing different individual students to have a turn at naming the letters as you point.

Tips for Teaching

[1] See Appendix pages 136 – 137 for The Alphabet Chant posters—one for upper-case letterforms and another for lower-case letterforms.

[2] Once students accurately and consistently name the upper-case letterforms, repeat the process with the Alphabet Chant chart for the lower-case letterforms.

[3] In this activity, the letter names are said not sung. The goal is to make a clear and explicit connection between individual letter symbols and their names. The purpose of the claps at designated points in the alphabet sequence is to avoid resorting to the familiar alphabet song, which can mask the one-to-one letter-to-name correspondences.

Phoneme-Grapheme Acquisition: Vowel Song (Stage 0)

Objective: To learn the common vowels sounds—short and long—for each vowel

Target students: Pre-K – K

Materials needed: An alphabet strip, the Vowel Song poster[1]

How to do activity:

1. Refer to the alphabet strip and identify the letters (a, e, i, o, and u) that represent the vowels. Explain to students that these are very important letters of the alphabet.
2. Display the Vowel Song poster.

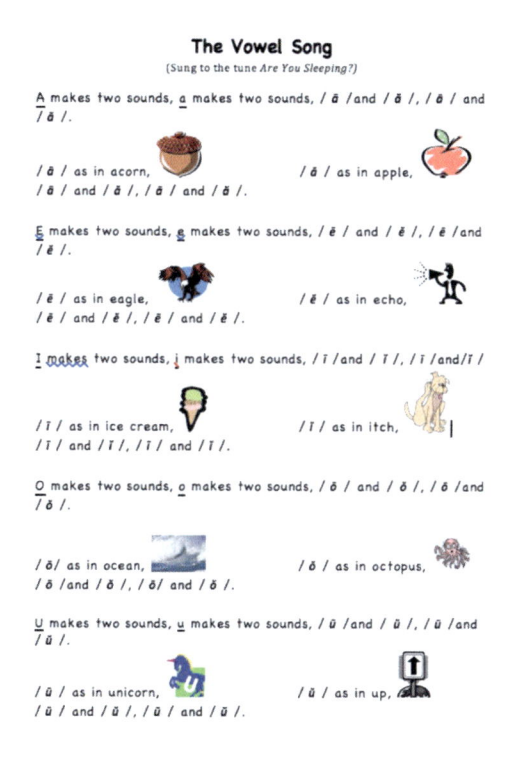

The Vowel Song
(Sung to the tune *Are You Sleeping?*)

A makes two sounds, a makes two sounds, / ā / and / ă /, / ā / and / ă /.

/ ā / as in acorn,   / ă / as in apple,
/ ā / and / ă /, / ā / and / ă /.

E makes two sounds, e makes two sounds, / ē / and / ĕ /, / ē / and / ĕ /.

/ ē / as in eagle,   / ĕ / as in echo,
/ ē / and / ĕ /, / ē / and / ĕ /.

I makes two sounds, i makes two sounds, / ī / and / ĭ /, / ī / and / ĭ /.

/ ī / as in ice cream,   / ĭ / as in itch,
/ ī / and / ĭ /, / ī / and / ĭ /.

O makes two sounds, o makes two sounds, / ō / and / ŏ /, / ō / and / ŏ /.

/ ō / as in ocean,   / ŏ / as in octopus,
/ ō / and / ŏ /, / ō / and / ŏ /.

U makes two sounds, u makes two sounds, / ū / and / ŭ /, / ū / and / ŭ /.

/ ū / as in unicorn,   / ŭ / as in up,
/ ū / and / ŭ /, / ū / and / ŭ /.

3. While pointing to the poster, sing the Vowel Song to the tune of *Are You Sleeping?*.
4. Repeat the song having students sing along with you as you point to the poster.
5. Invite individual or pairs of students to sing the song so that you can monitor their accuracy in producing the vowel sounds.
6. Repeat this activity daily allowing different individual or pairs of students to have a turn at singing the song.

Tips for Teaching

[1]See Appendix page 138 for The Vowel Song poster.

Phoneme-Grapheme Acquisition: See It...Say It...Write It (Stage 0)

Objective: To learn sound-letter associations for the letters of the alphabet including correct letter formations

Target students: Pre-K – K

Materials needed: Large cards (5 x 7 or 8 ½ x 11) with individual letters of the alphabet, wall cards with letters and key words for reference[1], white boards, markers, and erasers

How to do activity:

1. Give each student a white board, a marker, and eraser.
2. Show students a letter on a card. Explain that for each letter of the alphabet they will:
   a. See a letter and say the name of the letter (e.g., **b**)
   b. Say the sound associated with the letter (e.g., / *b* /)
   c. Write the letter

   When they do this, they will **See It...Say It...Write It**.
3. Model the process.
   - Display the letter card with the letter **b** (or the first letter in the scope and sequence being used[2]).
     - Say the name of the letter: **b**. Have student repeat the name.
     - Say the sound of the letter: / *b* /. Have students repeat the sound.
     - Skywrite the letter—using the correct letter formation[3]—while naming the letter. Have students skywrite the letter while naming the letter.
     - Have students write the letter **b** on their white boards using correct letter formation.
4. Practice the **See It...Say It...Write It** process with the current and previously taught letters to develop automaticity.

Tips for Teaching

[1]Teachers are encouraged to use references for letter formation that are provided as part of literacy programs they are using. If choosing their own key words, be careful to choose words that accurately cue the sound for the letter. For example, **x-ray** isn't a good choice for the letter **x** because it represents the name not the sound. A list of suggested key words appears in Appendix pages 139 - 141.

[2]Appendix 127 provides a suggested scope and sequence to teach letter-sound associations. If teachers use a program that provides a scope and sequence, they are encouraged to use it for consistency within the program.

[3]Appendix 142 provides an example of the stroke descriptions for continuous formation of manuscript letters. When teaching the formations, emphasize continuous strokes starting at the top and/or left side of the white board and moving to the bottom and/or right.

Phoneme-Grapheme Acquisition: Sound – Letter Maps (Stages 1 and 2)

Objective: To practice associating phonemes with graphemes

Target students: K – 3

Materials needed: Phoneme-Grapheme Map[1] or graph paper with numbered rows, tokens[2]; list of words[3]

How to do activity:[4]

1. Provide each student with a Phoneme-Grapheme Map, tokens, and a pencil.
2. Model the procedure as follows.
   a. First, identify the number of sounds in a word:
      i. Say a word on the list (e.g., **mat**)
      ii. Place one token per sound on the Phoneme-Grapheme Map (i.e., move one token for / m /, another for / ă /, and another for / t /)[5]

      iii. Identify the number of sounds in the word (3)
      iv. Point to each token and say the sound that corresponds from the word (/ m / / ă / / t /) and repeat the word (**mat**)
   b. Next, replace the token by writing the grapheme to represent each sound in the corresponding box. Name each letter aloud as you write it.
      i. Ask students: What sound do you hear? (/ m /)
      ii. Then ask: What letter(s) do you write? (m)

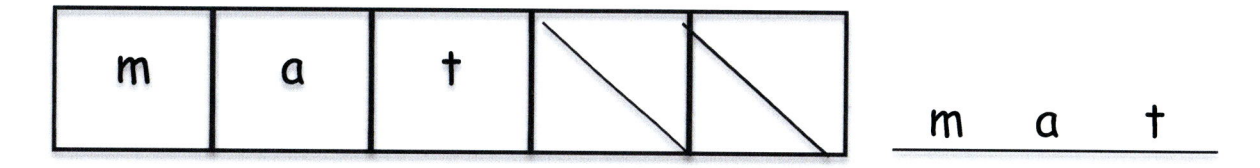

   c. Continue with other words on the list. Check that students are pronouncing the word correctly and synchronizing saying the sounds as they name and write each letter. Provide additional modeling of the task and immediate corrective feedback.
   d. Finally, have students write the letters for the word on the line to the right of the boxes to form the word. Be sure to have students read the whole word after they write it. At

the end, have students read the column of words to practice reading the words they just mapped.

[1] The Phoneme-Grapheme Map is a template to help students develop the sound-to-letter correspondences by making the process concrete. The map, composed of a row of five boxes, can be duplicated on paper for students and used with a document camera to model the process for students. See Appendix page 143 for a sample Phoneme-Grapheme Map.

[2] Tokens can be chips, magnets, cubes, or other types of manipulative objects that fit on the Phoneme-Grapheme Map.

[3] Follow the scope and sequence of sound/spelling associations used by the teacher, school or district. Doing this reinforces the sounds and ensures greater accuracy in doing the task. Within that scope and sequence, it is most effective to start with continuant sounds (e.g., / m /, / s /, / ă /) that have a one-to-one correspondence of sound to symbol (i.e., phoneme to grapheme).

[4] This activity builds upon the skill developed in the activity **Say It and Move It** in the Activities for Instruction and Informal Assessment section in *Phonemic Awareness: Knowledge to Practice* in the Literacy How Professional Development series.

[5] As students gain proficiency segmenting words with tokens, students can use their pencils to place a small dot in the boxes on the Phoneme-Grapheme Map rather than moving the tokens. This step ensures that students have processed the word phonemically before writing the letters for the sounds they hear.

Sound – Letter Maps should be used to reinforce the phoneme to grapheme relationships beyond those conditions where there is a one-to-one correspondence, including teaching phoneme–grapheme correspondences in which a speech sound can be represented by more than one letter (e.g., / ch / represented by **ch**; / ā / represented by **ai**). Consonant blends (e.g., **cl-**; **-st**) are also well-suited to **Sound-Letter Maps** because hearing each sound separately in the blend can be difficult for some students. The mapping process helps make the structure of blends concrete. Examples of maps for these types of phoneme-grapheme correspondences are illustrated below.

Consonant digraphs—one sound represented by two letters—write two letters in one box of the Phoneme-Grapheme Map. For example, for the word **chat**, the map would look like this with the first sound / ch / represented by the letters **c** + **h** in one box.

| ch | a | t | | |

Consonant blends—two sounds represented by two letters—write one letter per box. For the word **clap**, the letters are mapped with each letter of the blend (**cl-**) in its own box.[6]

c	l	a	p	

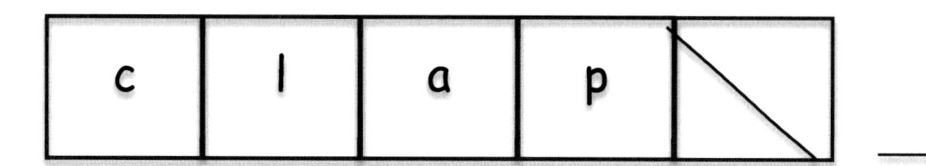

Silent e Pattern—one of the ways to represent a long vowel sound—maps each sound in a box. The role of the final **e** (i.e., silent **e**) is shown with a small **e** next to the final consonant letter, a signal that the first vowel sound / $\bar{a}$ / is long. This is the map for the word **grape**.

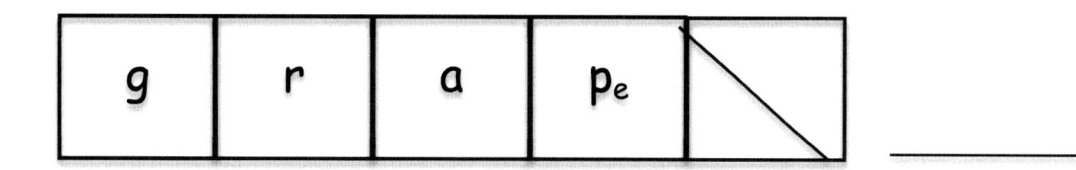

g	r	a	pe	

Vowel Teams—a long vowel sound represented by two letters—are represented with two letters in one box for one sound. For the word **rain**, the letters are mapped with the long / $\bar{a}$ / sound in one box.

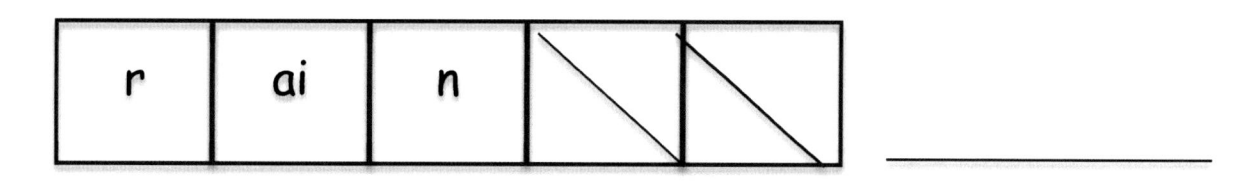

r	ai	n		

R-Controlled Vowels—vowel letter followed by **r**—are represented with two letters in one box for one sound. For the word **cart**, the letters are mapped with the r-controlled vowel / *ar* / in one box.

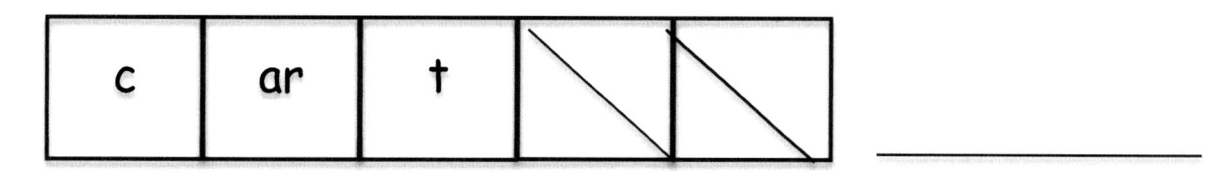

c	ar	t		

[6]When moving to more difficult sound sequences, such as words containing initial or final consonant combinations (i.e., blends), develop the sound segmentation skill by building from the rime. For example, begin with the rime (e.g., / ŏp /), add a consonant (e.g., / top /), and end with another consonant (e.g., / stop /). This approach is termed building from the "inside out." As students gain skill with blends this way, move to practice with blends building from the "outside in." For example, begin with / ăn /, add a consonant (e.g., / pan /), and end by inserting another consonant (e.g., / plan /).

Reading and Spelling Words

The following activities are designed to help students use letter-sound knowledge to read and spell words.

Domain: Phonics

Background information for this activity:

As students acquire knowledge of sound-letter associations and letter formation through explicit instruction, they also benefit from opportunities to practice using this knowledge in less-structured conditions. **Invented Writing** (See page 74) is designed to provide this practice. This is an activity in which approximations for conventional (i.e., correct orthographic spelling of words) are acceptable and encouraged. In this activity, students can employ invented spelling—that is, their closest written representation of the sounds they hear—as they continue to learn the correct orthographic representations. This practice helps students move from Stage 0 to Stage 1 as they form partial connections between salient letters and their corresponding sounds. Invented spelling, however, is not an end in spelling performance, but rather represents a transition from pre-alphabetic spelling to full-alphabetic knowledge. **Invented Writing** should be used in conjunction with **See It... Say It...Write It** to ensure students are learning these sound-letter associations correctly and systematically.

Dictating words, phrases, and sentences to students provides them with an opportunity to apply phonics knowledge to encoding. The selection of words and sentences is a critical aspect of this activity; it is essential to limit the selection of words to those composed of sound-letter correspondences that students have learned (See the **Listen and Write** activity page 76). Dictation practice using words with learned correspondences frees working memory so that students can focus on applying the encoding skills without juggling other aspects of writing, such as composing the sentences themselves. Like code-emphasis text to apply phonics to reading, a structured dictation provides targeted practice with the code to build automaticity in writing.

Corrective feedback is an essential component of the activity. By guiding students through a careful examination of misspellings, they become more aware of the orthographic patterns. Patterns of misspellings also provide teachers with insight about the need to reteach content and skills, as well as the focus and pacing of future instruction.

Reading words accurately and fluently requires that students master the skill of sound blending. Abundant practice manipulating sound-symbol associations to build and blend words contributes to this necessary skill development. Work with transparent sound-symbol associations, such as those found in closed syllable, open syllable, and silent e patterns, is particularly helpful to students who are learning to read (See the **Build and Blend** activity page 80).

The following table displays the activities designed to develop letter-sound knowledge to read and spell words across the stages.

Stage 0	Stage 1	Stage 2
Invented Writing (Use sound-symbol knowledge to encode words)	Listen and Write (Use letter-sound knowledge to write words) Build and Blend (Combine sounds into words)	Listen and Write (Use letter-sound knowledge to write words) Build and Blend (Combine sounds into words)

Reading and Spelling Words: Invented Writing (Stage 0)

Objective: To provide practice in applying knowledge of sound-letter associations and letter formation to spell words

Target students: Pre-K – K

Materials needed: Pictures[1], white paper, pencils, alphabet strips with key word pictures for each letter[2], and spacers[3]

How to do activity:

1. Provide each student with a picture for labeling, an alphabet strip, a piece of blank white paper, and a pencil. Have students place the alphabet strip on their desks or tables.
2. Model[4] the procedure as follows:
    a. Display and label a picture (e.g., **boat**)
    b. Tap out the sounds in the word and draw a line on a white board or piece of chart paper for each sound[5] (e.g., / b / / ō / / t / = 3 lines: ___ ___ ___).
    c. Have students make three lines on their pieces of paper.
    d. Repeat the label for the picture. Ask students to:
        i. Listen to the first sound,
        ii. Identify the letter that makes that sound,
        iii. Refer to the alphabet strip to help with letter formation, and
        iv. Write that letter for the first sound on the first line.
    e. Repeat these steps for the second and final sounds in the word.
    f. Ask students to 'read' the word that they wrote.
3. Encourage children to label their pictures, objects in the room, etc. using this technique.
4. As children progress to writing more than one word as they move to phrases or sentences, introduce 'spaceman' (i.e., spacer), which they insert between words.

Tips for Teaching

[1]Begin with pictures that represent one-syllable words (e.g., hat, snake, moon) and progress to multi-syllable words as students' skill increases

[2]Alphabet strips have the letters of the alphabet in order with a key picture for each letter. This is a reference that students use for information (e.g., invented writing) and formal (e.g., dictation) writing exercises

[3]A spacer is a clothespin or Popsicle stick to concretely represent the space between written words. This is easier for many students than using a finger between words.

[4]The teacher guides the process but the student is doing the writing. Initially, the teacher models the analysis of sounds in the words. After that, the encoding shifts to the students. Through this process, students might use the letter **o**, or **oa**, or **o_e** to represent long / ō /, which is what makes it

"invented." In this way, teachers can see the extent to which students have mastered conventional spelling. In this activity, teachers do not typically present students with the correct spelling unless students have been taught the orthographic pattern and are expected to use the correct (i.e., conventional) spelling.

[5] As students become more proficient, you may remove the scaffold of having a line to represent each sound in the word.

Reading and Spelling Words: Listen and Write (Stage 1)

Objective: To apply sound-letter knowledge (phonics) to write words and sentences.

Target students: K – 2[1]

Materials needed: Individual white boards, lined composition paper, or writing notebook; pencils with erasers, tokens, preplanned list of words and sentences selected from the decodable text that students have recently read[2]

How to do activity:

1. Provide students with a piece of lined composition paper or their writing notebook, a pencil and tokens.
2. Follow this procedure with three to five words that represent a phonetic pattern that the students have recently learned.
    a. Say one of the words and have the students repeat the word (e.g., **blast**).
    b. Have students finger spell or tap the sounds in the word to preview the spelling of the word[3].
    c. Have students write each word synchronizing saying the sound with the letter or letters for each sound.
    d. Check as students write each word and give immediate corrective feedback. For example, if they write **bast**, ask them to read what they wrote and listen for the difference between their response and the target word. If they have difficulty, ask them to say the sound for each letter they wrote, and blend it together. Again, prompt students to listen to the difference between their written response (**bast**) and the target word (**blast**). This type of careful examination helps students identify their errors.
3. Next, follow this procedure with sentences selected from the text that students recently read[4].
    a. Dictate a complete sentence and ask students to repeat the sentence.
    b. Have students repeat the sentence and place a token above their paper for each word in the sentence[5]. Prompt students to use the row of tokens as a reference, if they have difficulty remembering the sentence.
    c. After students write the sentence, ask them to read what they wrote. Some students will leave out a word and when they read the sentence back, they discover the omission and insert the missing word.
    d. If a student writes a word incorrectly but reads the word as you dictated it, use the same corrective feedback as before. Specifically, ask them to say the sounds for the letters and blend the sounds in the word that they spelled incorrectly to encourage self-correction.[6]

Tips for Teaching

[1]This activity is best used in a small, guided reading groups with the students' spelling data as a starting point to tailor the words for dictation. For example, if students have difficult spelling final blends, select words with that pattern.

[2]Selecting words, phrases, or sentences from decodable text reading selections that students have read increases the likelihood that students will be able to spell (encode) the words.

[3]Some students will benefit from a preliminary warm-up step. Writing letters that represent dictated sounds that they will use in dictated words can help prepare students to spell the whole words. Again, select targeted phonetic features as well as those features that students continue to misspell.

[4]Begin with two-word sentences (e.g., **Sam sat**.) Gradually increase the number of words in the sentence as students demonstrate that they can remember the sentence and accurately encode the words. If it is necessary to continually repeat the sentence, cut back on the number of words in the sentence.

[5]This may not be necessary for all students but is helpful for those who have difficulty remembering a long complex sentence.

[6]You may periodically want to use this activity as an informal diagnostic assessment. Spelling errors can be analyzed to determine what spelling patterns the students are using but confusing.

Reading and Spelling Words: Listen and Write (Stage 2)

Objective: To apply sound-letter and advanced phonics knowledge to write words and sentences.

Target students: 2 – 3[1]

Materials needed: Individual white boards, lined composition paper, or writing notebook; pencils with erasers, tokens, preplanned list of words and sentences selected from decodable or authentic text that students have recently read that adhere to more advanced levels of the phonics scope and sequence and other aspects of advanced phonics[2]

How to do activity:

1. Provide students with a piece of lined composition paper or their writing notebook, a pencil and tokens.
2. Follow this procedure with three to five words that represent a phonetic or syllabic pattern that the students have recently learned.
    a. Say one of the words and have the students repeat the word (e.g., **orbit**).
    b. Have students finger spell or tap the sounds in the word to preview the spelling of the word[3]. For multi-syllable words, adjust this process to spell each syllable in the word (e.g., **or, bit**).
    c. Have students write each word or syllable synchronizing saying the sound with the letter or letters for each sound.
    d. Check as students write each word and give immediate corrective feedback.[4]
3. Next, follow this procedure with sentences selected from the text that students recently read[5].
    a. Dictate a complete sentence and ask students to repeat the sentence. Demonstrate saying the sentence in meaningful phrases to facilitate recall.
    b. After students write the sentence, ask them to read what they wrote. Some students will leave out a word and when they read the sentence back, they discover the omission and insert the missing word.
    c. If a student writes a word incorrectly but reads the word as you dictated it, use the same corrective feedback as before. Specifically, ask them to say the sounds for the letters and blend the sounds in the word or syllable that they spelled incorrectly to encourage self-correction.[6]

Tips for Teaching

[1]This activity is best used in a small, guided reading groups with the students' spelling data as a starting point to tailor the words for dictation, particularly with regards to the scope and sequence of phonics. For example, if students have difficult spelling two-syllable words, select words with that pattern.

[2]Selecting words, phrases, or sentences from decodable text reading selections that students have read increases the likelihood that students will be able to spell (encode) the words. (For more on advanced phonics see page 49).

[3]The words to practice in step 2 should be selected from the sentences that will be dictated in step 3. For the example of this activity, the sentences have been selected from *Explore Our Solar System*: **Eight planets orbit, or revolve around, the sun. The planets and the sun are parts of our solar system.**

[4]When spelling multi-syllable words, students may experience difficulty spelling the vowel in unaccented syllables. For example, when spelling the word **solar** (/sō lər/), students may spell the unaccented syllable **ler**. Corrective feedback should include a reminder about the schwa sound and a focus on the correct vowel letter to use. For more on schwa, see the activity **Schwallowed Vowels** page 102.

[5]Begin with two-word sentences that emphasize a specific phonetic or syllable pattern (e.g., **Planets orbit**.). Gradually increase the number of words in the sentence as students demonstrate that they can remember the sentence and accurately encode the words. Select sentences directly from the text as students are able to negotiate more words and encoding demands. If it is necessary to continually repeat the sentence, cut back on the number of words in the sentence.

[6]You may periodically want to use this activity as an informal diagnostic assessment. Spelling errors can be analyzed to determine what spelling patterns the students are using but confusing.

Reading and Spelling Words: Build and Blend (Stage 1 and 2)

Objective: To practice blending phonemes together to read words

Target students: K – 3

Materials needed: Large cards (5 x 7 or 8 ½ x 11) with lower case letter(s) including single consonants, single vowels and consonant digraphs, preplanned word lists[1]

How to do activity:

1. Distribute letter cards—one per student—according to the words on the preplanned word list.
2. Have the students take turns saying the name and sound for their letters. If a child has difficulty remembering the sound, prompt with its key word (e.g., apple for / ă /).
3. Say a word from the preplanned Closed Syllable word list (e.g., **mat**). Have students identify the sounds in the word (e.g., / m / / ă / / t /).
4. Ask students who have the letters that represent these sounds to come to the front of the class and build the word (e.g., **m – a – t**). Use the cue "Build It."
5. Stand behind the students with the letters. Tap each letter-holder on the head as they say the sound their letter makes (e.g., / m / / ă / / t /). Say "Blend It" to have students combine the sounds to say the word (e.g., **mat**). Have students hold hands or link arms as they blend the sounds together and say the word.
6. Repeat with the next word on the preplanned list of words utilizing the letters that the students have for building.

Variations:
- For students who need more explicit, scaffolded instruction, begin with a rime (e.g., **at**) and add different onsets to build new words (e.g., **mat, cat, sat, rat, bat**, and so on). Have students build the rime in front of the class. Say a word with that rime pattern. Ask the student with the beginning sound to join the rime in the front of the class.

- Word chains/minimal pairs: Have students determine the sound-letter association that changes. Students with the letters that change trade places. For example: build **map** from **mat**, **cap** from **map**, **mop** from **map**.

- When students are accurate and automatic building and blending CVC words, expand the activity to include initial (CCVC) and final (CVCC) consonant blends. For example, build **trap** from **tap** and **bend** from **bed**. Then move to CCVCC words. For example, build **blend** from **bend** and **bed**.

- **Build and Blend...*then* Write It**: After **Build and Blend**, have all students **Write It** on individual white boards or have a scribe write the words on a whiteboard at the front of the classroom. This provides students with additional practice reading the words that they have built.

- Practice contrasting closed and open vowel patterns by removing the final consonant in words (e.g., **got** to **go**, **met** to **me**, **him** to **hi**, **nod** to **no**, and so on). Use this in conjunction with **Syllable Inspectors** (See this activity page 84).

- Contrast closed and silent e patterns by adding a 'magic e' to the end of words (e.g., **tap** to **tape**, **pet** to **Pete**, **fin** to **fine**, **not** to **note**, **cut** to **cute**). For this variation, add a Magic **e** Wand to the materials list. One child is selected to hold the Magic **e** Wand. When the magic **e** is added to the end of a closed syllable word, the Magic **e** Wand taps the vowel in front of it signaling that the vowel now says its long sound. Use this in conjunction with **Syllable Inspectors** (See this activity page 84).

Tips for Teaching

[1]Preplanned word lists, based on the targeted syllable type(s), make this activity easier. Here are sample lists for closed, open, and silent e syllables with the letters cards needed to build them.

Closed: **mat, bat, sat, mad, sad, bad, bid, sit, bit, did** (Letter cards: **m, b, a, t, s, d, i**)
Open: **hi, my, try, he, she, cry, go, so** (Letter cards: **h, m, y, t, r, sh, c, g, s, e, i, o,**)
Silent e: **bake, make, lake, bike, Mike, like, fine, fake, mane, mine** (Letter cards: **b, m, l, a, e, k, i, f, n**)

Syllable Pattern Identification

The following activities focus the conditions that characterize the six types of syllables to facilitate syllable identification and pronunciation skills to help students read and spell multi-syllable words.

Domain: Phonics

Background information for this activity:

Most words in English are composed of one or a combination of six syllable types. The syllable types are distinguished by the position or pattern of the vowel (V), which indicates how the vowel sound is pronounced. The six syllable types are:

Syllable type	Pattern	Vowel sound	Examples
Closed	VC	Short vowel	at, Ed, it, on, up
	VCV		cap, bit, pet, tot, cut
Open	CV	Long vowel	be, I, my
Silent e	VCe	Long vowel	cape, bite, Pete, tote, cute
Vowel Teams • Talkers • Whiners	VV	Long vowel Vowel sound is neither long nor sort but a different sound called a diphthong	rain, boat boil, boy
R-controlled	Vr	Vowel sound is neither long nor short but is influenced by r that follows the vowel letter	far, for, her, fir fur
Consonant-le	C-le	Vowel sound is schwa	can*dle*, ta*ble*, gur*gle*

Knowledge of the syllable types helps readers know how to pronounce the vowel sound within the combination of letters (See the **Syllable Inspectors** activity page 84).

Categorization has benefits for both students and teachers. By categorizing syllables, students develop greater accuracy and automaticity in recognizing the vowel patterns and the corresponding pronunciation (See the **Syllable Sort** activity page 97). Through categorizing syllables, teachers can observe the degree to which their students have learned to identify the targeted patterns. Student performance in sorting syllables into categories informs the need for additional instruction or practice so that students become accurate and automatic in recognizing the patterns.

Any discussion of syllables in multi-syllable words must include understanding of the schwa sound. Schwa is an unaccented vowel occurring in the unaccented syllable of multi-syllable words. The vowel is less clear—like it is being swallowed—so, we can think of the schwa as "*schwa*llowed" vowels. The schwa, which sounds similar to short **u** or short **i**, accounts for about 20% of the vowels spoken (See the *Schwa*llowed **Vowels** activity page 102).

Accent (i.e., the stressed syllable in a multi-syllable word) and schwa are related. For this reason, it is important to recognize accent in order to understand schwa. A few guidelines help to identify the unaccented (i.e., unstressed) syllables:

- In two-syllable words, often the second syllable is unstressed (e.g., pen*cil*, bas*ket*, ta*ble*)
- Prefixes and suffixes are often unstressed (e.g., *re*turn, want*ed*, plant*ing*)
- The letter "a" at the beginning of end of a word (e.g., *a*bove, *a*round, pand*a*)
- In multi-syllable words of more than two syllables, the middle syllable is often unstressed (e.g., com*pe*tent, bal*co*ny, int*er*est)

Notice that in each of the unaccented syllables, the expected short or long sound for the vowel is reduced to schwa, which sounds like / ŭ / or / ĭ /.

The following table displays the activities designed to develop syllable identification and pronunciation skills across Stages 1 and 2.

Stage 0	Stage 1	Stage 2
	Syllable Inspectors (Use vowel pattern knowledge to identify syllable types) Syllable Sort (Categorize syllables based on type)	Syllable Inspectors (Use vowel pattern knowledge to identify syllable types) Syllable Sort (Categorize syllables based on type) *Schwa*llowed Vowels (Learn the role of the schwa sound in multi-syllable words)

Syllable Pattern Identification: Syllable Inspectors (Stages 1 and 2)

Objective: To distinguish syllable types based on the vowel position or pattern

Target students: K – 3

Materials needed: Pre-planned words for the syllable type being introduced written on cards[1], vowel posters, rule cards for syllable types[2], and magnifying glass—real or pretend

How to do activity:

This activity—**Syllable Inspectors**—is designed to teach students to "inspect" letter patterns to determine the pronunciation of the vowel sound. Introduce each syllable pattern with the following basic steps:

1. Tell students that they are going to inspect words to learn what sound to say for the vowel letter(s) in them. Knowing how to inspect the vowel and the consonant(s) that may come after the vowel helps us read and spell new words.
2. Review the vowels sounds (e.g., short, long, r-controlled) that are the focus of the targeted syllable pattern for the lesson[3].
3. Display a word as a model of the pattern. Use the magnifying glass to inspect the word to identify the pattern of letters to determine the position—and therefore the sound—represented by the vowel letter(s).
4. Tell the Syllable Story that describes the pattern of letters that we see and the vowel sound that we hear.
5. Post the syllable pattern rule card for the specific pattern you are teaching. Review the characteristics on the rule card while using the model word to illustrate how it works.
6. Practice with additional words from the pre-planned list of words.
7. Sort words/syllables according to their syllable types as a way to check for understanding of the targeted patterns.

Tips for Teaching

[1]Introduction of the syllable types should be systematic and cumulative based on a scope and sequence.

[2]Rule cards for each syllable type are available in the Appendix on pages 149 – 156.

[3]Lessons should only include those syllable types that have been previously taught and mastered before introducing another pattern.

Closed syllables

The pre-planned words to introduce the Closed Syllable pattern include:

Closed syllables—**at, cat, mat, sat, mast, map, dad, sad, mad, it, sit, did, in, tin, dim, mint, mist, sis, hat, hit, him, had, hid, hit, tint**

Non-closed syllables—**see, too, be, my, I**

1. Tell students that they are going to inspect—that is, look closely at—some words to learn why the vowel sounds say their short sound. Knowing how to inspect the vowel in words helps us read and spell new words.

2. Review the short sounds for the vowels using the vowel posters and gestures to cue those sounds: **apple** - / ă /, **itch** - / ĭ /, **echo** - / ĕ /, **octopus** - / ŏ /, **up** - / ŭ /.

3. Display the word **cat**. Have students identify the vowel sound (/ ă / as in **apple**). Display the word **in**. Have students identify the vowel sound (/ ĭ / as in **itch**).

4. Use the magnifying glass to inspect the word and discuss the conditions that make the vowel sound short. Tell the story for Closed Syllables:

    When one vowel is followed by one or more consonants, the vowel sound is usually short. When we **see** these conditions in a word, the vowel sound we **hear** is usually short.

5. Show the syllable pattern rule card for Closed Syllables. Review the characteristics on the rule card while using the model word (**cat**) to illustrate how it works.

6. Display other closed syllable words from the pre-planned list. Have students take turns using the magnifying glass to inspect each word to see if the word follows the pattern for a closed syllable. Continue until students are accurately and consistently recognizing that the words have one vowel followed by at least one consonant. Explain that these are closed syllables—the vowel is closed in by the consonant at the end.

7. Display **see**. Inspect the word to determine if it follows the pattern for a closed syllable. Help students to see that **see** has two vowel letters and no consonant after the vowels. The word **see** doesn't follow the pattern for a closed syllable.

8. Pass out closed syllable and non-closed syllable word cards to the students. Practice being Syllable Inspectors to decide if each word is a closed syllable word or not. Sort the words on a bulletin board, pocket chart or into columns on the floor or table as either closed syllables and non-closed syllables.

9. After all of the words are sorted, read the list of closed syllable words and review the closed syllable conditions-- one vowel with one or more consonants after the vowel. When we see these conditions in a word, the vowel sound is usually short.

Open syllables

The pre-planned words to introduce the Open Syllable pattern include:
met (me), **not** (no), **got** (go), **bet** (be), **hit** (hi).
- The words should be written on index cards or strips of paper so that the final letter (see shaded box in #5 below) can be folded back after the vowel to change from the closed to the open syllable pattern (e.g., **met** becomes **me** when the **t** is folded back).
- Make two of each card—one that will be left as a closed syllable and one that will be folded back to create an open syllable.

1. Tell students that they are going to continue to be Syllable Inspectors to learn what the vowel sounds are in words.
2. Review the short and long sounds for the vowels: **apple** - / ă /, **itch** - / ĭ /, **echo** - / ĕ /, **octopus** - / ŏ /, **up** - / ŭ /; **acorn** - / ā /, **eagle** / ē /, **ice cream** - / ī /, **ocean** - / ō /, **unicorn** - / ū /.
3. Review the conditions for a closed syllable: one vowel with one or more consonants after the vowel. When we see these conditions in a word, the vowel sound is usually short.
4. Display the word **met**. Have students inspect the word to determine if it is a closed syllable. Tell the story to review the conditions for Closed Syllables.

| m | e | t |

5. Fold the **t** back on the duplicate card of the word **met**. Use the magnifying glass to inspect the word and discuss the conditions that make the vowel sound long. Tell the story for Open Syllables:

    When one vowel letter is at the end of a syllable with NO consonants after it, the vowel sound is long. When we **see** these conditions in a word, the vowel sound we **hear** is usually long.

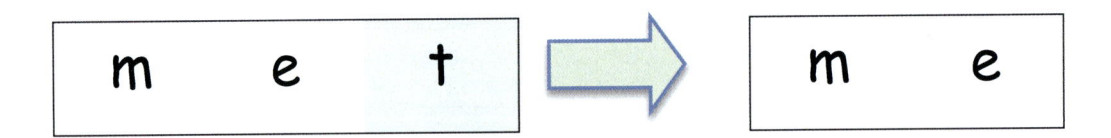

| m | e | t | ⇒ | m | e |

6. Show the syllable pattern rule card for Open Syllables. Review the characteristics on the rule card while using the model word (**met**) to illustrate how it works.

7. Illustrate the change from closed to open syllable with another one of the words on the pre-planned cards. Continue with the remaining pre-planned cards having students use the magnifying glass to be Syllable Inspectors.

8. Sort the words on a bulletin board, pocket chart or into columns on the floor or table as either closed syllables or open syllables.

9. After all of the words are sorted, read the list of closed syllable words and review the conditions for closed syllables—one vowel with one or more consonants after the vowel. When we see these conditions in a word, the vowel sound is usually short. Review conditions for open syllables—one vowel with NO consonants after the vowel. The vowel sound is usually long.

Silent e Syllable

The pre-planned words to introduce the Silent e Syllable pattern include:
cap – cape, **bit** – bite, **pet** – Pete, **tot** – tote, **cut** – cute.

Another set of words to practice the relationship between Closed and Silent e Syllables:
at – ate, **tap** – tape, **hop** – hope, **us** – use, **rid** – ride

Additional Silent e Syllable words:
make, bake, hike, tame, came, late, cube, kite, time, here

Index card with "e" written on it

1. Tell students that they are going to continue to be Syllable Inspectors to learn what the vowel sounds are in words.

2. Review the short and long sounds for the vowels: **apple** - / ă /, **itch** - / ĭ /, **echo** - / ĕ /, **octopus** - / ŏ /, **up** - / ŭ /; **acorn** - / ā /, **eagle** / ē /, **ice cream** - / ī /, **ocean** - / ō /, **unicorn** - / ū /.

3. Use the Syllable Rule Card to review the conditions for Closed Syllable: one vowel with one or more consonants after the vowel. When we see these conditions in a word, the vowel sound is usually short.

4. Display the word **cap**. Have students inspect the word to determine if it is a Closed Syllable. Review the story for Closed syllables.

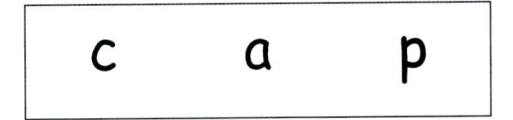

| c | a | p |

5. Place the index card with the letter "e" at the end of the word and say the word **cape**. Use the magnifying glass to inspect the word and discuss the impact of adding the letter "e" at the end. Tell the story for the Silent e Syllable:

   When a word has a vowel followed by a consonant followed by a final **e**, the **e** at the end signals the other vowel to say its name—it's long sound. The final **e** gives away its power, so it is silent. When we **see** these conditions in a word, the vowel sound we **hear** is usually long.

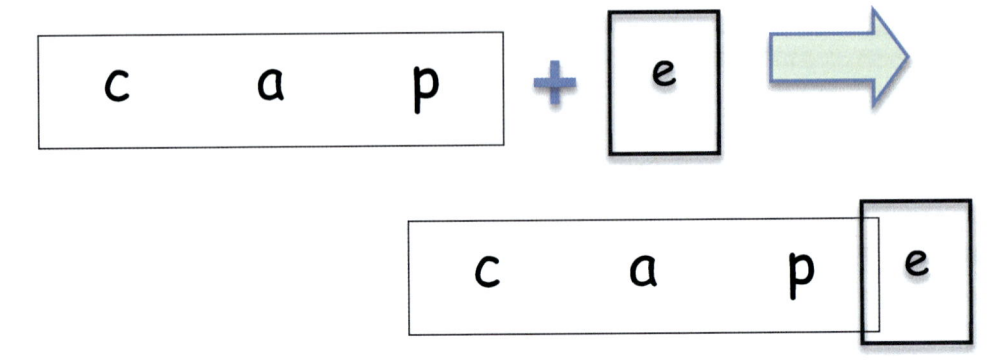

| c | a | p | + | e | ➡ |

| c | a | p | e |

88

6. Show the syllable pattern rule card for the Silent e Syllable. Review the characteristics on the rule card while using the model word (**cape**) to illustrate how it works.

7. Illustrate the change from Closed to Silent **e** Syllable with another one of the word pairs on the pre-planned cards. Continue with the remaining pre-planned cards having students use the magnifying glass to be Syllable Inspectors.

8. Sort the words on a bulletin board, pocket chart or into columns on the floor or table as either Closed Syllables or Silent e Syllables.

9. After all of the words are sorted, read the list of Closed Syllable words and review the conditions for Closed Syllables—one vowel with one or more consonants after the vowel. When we see these conditions in a word, the vowel sound is usually short. Review conditions for Silent **e** Syllables—when one vowel is followed by a consonant and then an "e," the first vowel sound is usually long and the final "**e**" is silent.

Vowel Team Syllables

Vowel Teams are divided into two groups—each with a distinctive difference.

- The vowel sound in one group of vowel teams is the long sound (i.e., the name of the first vowel). These vowel teams include: **ai**, **ay**, **ee**, **ea**, **ie**, **oe**, **ow** (/ ō /), **ui**, and **ue**. For instructional purposes, this group is called "**Talkers**" because the first vowel says its name.

- In the other group of vowel teams, the vowel sound is neither short nor long but different; this group of vowel teams is called diphthongs. These vowel teams include: **ow**, **au**, **aw**, **oi**, **oy**, **oo** (boo and book), **ew**. The sounds represented by these vowel teams are whiney sounds, so this group is called "**Whiners**."

To help students learn words in each group. Introduce them separately and practice them until students recognize the words in one group (e.g., **Talkers**) before introducing the other group (e.g., **Whiners**). This is especially important for the purpose of spelling. It can be confusing to introduce too many teams at the same time.

Preplanned words to introduce Vowel Teams – Talkers:
rain, train, brain, faint, paint; say, stay, pay, gray, tray; tree, bee, see, free, green, seem; tie, pie, lie; toe, doe, Joe; mow, blow, snow, glow; suit, fruit; blue, glue, true

1. Tell students that they are going to inspect some words to learn another way that vowels look when they say their long sounds. Knowing how to inspect the vowels in words helps us read and spell new words.

2. Review the long sounds for the vowels using the vowel posters to cue these sounds: **acorn** - / ā /, **eagle** / ē /, **ice cream** - / ī /, **ocean** - / ō /, **unicorn** - / ū /.

3. Display and say the word **rain**. Have students identify the vowel sound (/ ā / as in **acorn**).

4. Use the magnifying glass to inspect the word and discuss the conditions that make the vowel say its long sound. Tell the story for the Talkers on the Vowel Team:

    When we see two vowels side-by-side in a word, sometimes the first one says its name, which is the long sound. When we **see** these conditions, the vowel sound we **hear** is usually long.

5. Show the syllable pattern rule card for Vowel Team – Talkers. Review the characteristics on the rule card while using the model word (**rain**) to illustrate how it works.

6. Display other Vowel Team – Talkers words. Have students take turns using the magnifying glass to inspect each word to see if the word follows the pattern for a Vowel Team – Talker. Continue until students are accurately and consistently recognizing that the words that have two vowel letters side-by-side say the name of the first vowel letter. This is the long sound.

Preplanned words to introduce <u>Vowel Teams—Whiners</u>:
now, **how**, **cow**, **howl**, **plow**, **growl**; **fault**, **vault**, **maul**, **auto**; **saw**, **raw**, **paw**, **claw**; **oil**, **boil**, **soil**, **spoil**;
boy, **soy**, **toy**, **ploy**; **boo**, **soon**, **spoon**, **fool**, **pool**; **book**, **look**, **cook**, **took**

1. Tell students that they are going to inspect some words to learn another sound for Vowel Teams. Knowing how to inspect the vowels in words helps us read and spell new words.

2. Review the short and long sounds for the vowels: **apple** - / ă /, **itch** - / ĭ /, **echo** - / ĕ /, **octopus** - / ŏ /, **up** - / ŭ /; **acorn** - / ā /, **eagle** / ē /, **ice cream** - / ī /, **ocean** - / ō /, **unicorn** - / ū /. Explain that there are some Vowel Teams that say very different sounds, called diphthongs. Diphthong sounds aren't long or short.

3. Display and say the word **now**. Have students identify the vowel sound (/ ow /). Point out that the letter **o** isn't saying its name (/ ō /) or short sound (/ ŏ /).

4. Use the magnifying glass to inspect the word and discuss the conditions that make the vowel say this different sound. Tell the story for the Whiners on the Vowel Team:

    Sometimes when we see two vowels side-by-side in a word, they make a funny whining sound, like when you fall down and say "ow," "aw," and "oi." When we **see** these conditions, the vowel sound we **hear** may be a whiny one.

5. Show the syllable pattern rule card for Vowel Team – Whiners. Review the characteristics on the rule card while using the model word (**now**) to illustrate how it works.

6. Display other Vowel Team – Whiner words. Have students take turns using the magnifying glass to inspect each word to see if the word follows the pattern for a Vowel Team – Whiner. Continue until students are accurately and consistently recognizing that these words that have two vowel letters side-by-side say the diphthong, that is whiny, sound.

After students are reading each group of Vowel Team words accurately (i.e., the **Talker** group and the **Whiner** group), mix together the words from the preplanned cards from both groups. Have students sort the words into the **Talkers** and the **Whiners**.

R-controlled (Bossy r) Syllable

The pre-planned words to introduce the R-controlled Syllable pattern include:
- ar—rat - art, ram - arm, car, star, cart, bar, dart, part, chart, shark, hard, yard
- or—rob - orb (use this pair for introduction); **or, cord, corn, born, horn, morn, torn, for, fort**
- er—**her, fern, clerk**
- ir—**fir, first, skirt**
- ur—**fur, turn, hurt**

Index card with "r" written on it

1. Tell students that they are going to continue to be Syllable Inspectors to learn what the vowel sounds are in words they read and spell.

2. Review the long sounds for the vowels **acorn** - / ā /, **eagle** / ē /, **ice cream** - / ī /, **ocean** - / ō /, **unicorn** - / ū / and the short sounds for the vowels **apple** - / ă /, **itch** - / ĭ /, **echo** - / ĕ /, **octopus** - / ŏ /, **up** - / ŭ /.

3. Display the letter **r**. Explain that sometimes **r** partners with vowels. Tell the story of how **r** came to work with the vowels:

    > **R** wanted to be important like the vowels and wished his name could be a sound heard in words too. **R** had an idea. It offered to help the vowels. The vowels were worried because the **r** was fond of being bossy.

    (Write the word **rat** on the board or a piece of chart paper.)

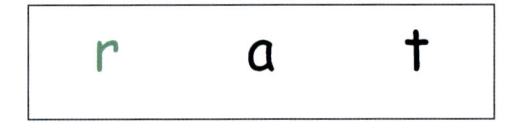

    | r | a | t |

4. Continue the story about how the **r** came to work with the vowels:

    > The vowel **a** was especially doubtful, she said, "I smell a rat!" But **r** didn't give up. "I really want to be helpful, so he offered to let the vowel be first in words.

    (Write the word **art** next to the word **rat** emphasizing the order of the letters **a** and **r**.)

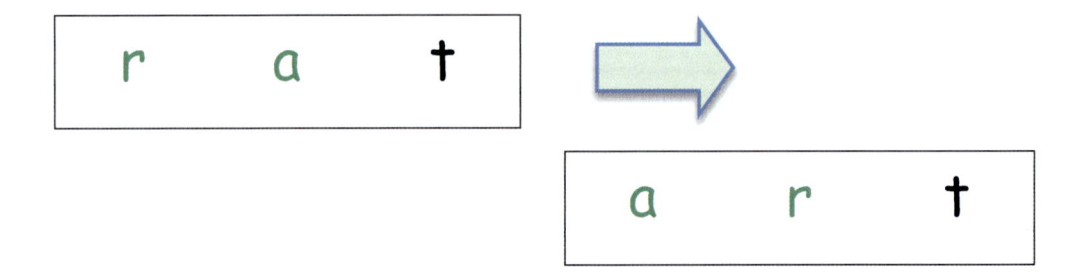

    | r | a | t | ➡ | a | r | t |

Sure enough, as soon as **a** moved in front of **r** she noticed she could no longer say her short sound. Instead, she said something completely unexpected… / *ar* /. "What's going on?" she asked. "I can't even hear myself anymore. In fact, all I hear is your name **r**." **R** just smiled.

Then **a** said, "I've heard enough. I'm leaving." Suddenly **r** realized that with the **a** gone there was no long a word (**rt**). Every word needs a vowel. **R** couldn't say its name unless **a** came before him. **R** had to think of a way to get **a** to stay.

R said, "Together we've made a completely new vowel sound… / *ar* /. Together we can make lots of new words: **far**, **star**, **cart** (write these words on the board or chart paper).

A was happy because she found that she could be part of the new sound with **r** and still have her short sound if she changed position to come after **r** (**art** to **rat**).

5. Show the syllable pattern rule card for the R-controlled Syllable. Review the characteristics on the rule card: The r is bossy and takes over the sound of the vowel. The vowel can't say its short or long sound, but says a sound with the r.
6. Illustrate the change from Closed to R-controlled with another preplanned words for ar (ram). Illustrate how reversing the order of the letters r and a, the word becomes arm.
7. Continue with the remaining pre-planned cards having students use the magnifying glass to look for the ar combination. Be sure to have students practice saying the sound / ar /.

Follow the same procedure to introduce the other r-controlled vowels patterns and corresponding sounds: **or** (/ *or* /); **er, ir, ur** (/ *er* /)[1]. Use the syllable pattern rule card for the R-controlled Syllable to review the letter patterns and corresponding pronunciations. Use the following story to explain why there are only three bossy r sounds even though there are five vowels. Continue the story about how the **r** came to work with the vowels.

The vowel **o** was also lucky and got to form a new vowel sound that is also a word – **or**. Naturally the remaining vowels **e, i,** and **u** pestered **r** for a chance to pair up to create a new vowel sound. By now **r** began to realize that with increased importance comes more work. He was tired! Finally, **r** announced he would only make one additional sound--/ *er* /. The remaining vowels were left to figure out who would get the last sound. After a lot of bickering, they concluded it was only fair to share the / *er* / sound, which is why **er, ir,** and **ur** all sound the same.

Tips for Teaching

[1]There are three spellings for the / er / sound: **er**, **ir**, **ur**. Unfortunately, there are no rules to help choose the correct spelling. The recommendation is to choose **er** first because it is the most frequently used of the three spellings, followed by **ir** and finally **ur**. Be sure to provide abundant practice with each / er / spelling in lists and text to foster sight recognition of the words.

Consonant – le Syllable

The Consonant – le Syllable is always the final syllable in a multi-syllable word—it never stands alone as a word therefore this type of syllable always joins with another type of syllable to make a word. For this reason, the preplanned word lists for Syllable Inspector are organized according to the first syllable in the words—Closed, Open, or R-controlled; the second (final) syllable in each word is the Consonant – le Syllable.

The preplanned words to introduce the Closed + Consonant - le Syllable pattern include:
can**dle**, han**dle**, sim**ple**, un**cle**, bub**ble**, jun**gle** (Write each syllable on a separate card—**can** + **dle**, and so on.)

The preplanned words to introduce the Open + Consonant - le Syllable pattern include:
ta**ble**, cra**dle**, ti**tle**, fa**ble**, i**dle** (Write each syllable on a separate card—ta + **ble**, and so on.)

The preplanned words to introduce the R-controlled + Consonant - le Syllable pattern include:
mar**ble**, gur**gle**, pur**ple**, spar**kle**, hur**dle** (Write each syllable on a separate card— mar + **ble**, and so on.)

To introduce the Consonant – le Syllable pattern, focus on one of the preplanned word lists at a time.

1. Tell students that they are going to continue to be Syllable Inspectors to learn what the vowel sounds are in words they read and spell. Explain that the next syllable pattern is very unusual because it is always combined with another type of syllable to make a longer (i.e., multi-syllable) word.

2. Display the first syllable in **candle** (**can**). Review the story for Closed Syllables: When one vowel is followed by one or more consonants after the vowel, the vowel sound is usually short. When we see these conditions in a word, the vowel sound we hear is usually short. Have students read the syllable.

| c | a | n |

3. Display the second syllable in **candle** (**dle**). Say the syllable for the students and explain that the vowel sound they hear is between the consonant (**d**) and the **le**, but you don't see the sound you hear. Tell the story for the Consonant - le Syllable:

When you see a **consonant** + **l** + **e** as the last syllable in a word, the vowel in the syllable doesn't sound like a short or long vowel sound. The "l" bosses the syllable and makes the **e** silent.

| c | a | n | | d | l | e |

4. Show the syllable pattern rule card for the Consonant -le Syllable. Review the characteristics on the rule card while using the model word to illustrate how it works.
5. Continue to display the two syllables that make up the words on the preplanned word list. Guide students to inspect each syllable to determine the pattern to know how to say the vowel sound.
6. Follow the same procedure to introduce the other combination of syllables (e.g., Open, R-controlled) with Consonant -le and corresponding sounds.

Syllable Pattern Identification: Syllable Sort (Stage 1)

Objective: To practice vowel pattern (syllable types) categorization

Target students: K – 2

Materials needed: Pre-planned syllables for at least two syllable types for the sort written on cards[1, 2], vowel posters, and rule cards for syllable types that are targeted for the sort

How to do activity:

This activity – Syllable Sort—can be used as soon as students have learned two of the syllable types.

Follow these basic steps to guide students through the sorting process:

1. Tell students that they are going to sort syllables to practice inspecting the vowel and the consonant(s) that may come after the vowel. Being able to do this helps them read and spell words.
2. Review the vowels sounds (e.g., short and long) that are the focus of the targeted syllable pattern for the lesson.
3. Review the syllable pattern rule cards and related Syllable Stories that correspond to the types of syllables that are the focus of the sort (e.g., Closed and Silent **e**)

Closed: VC CCVC CVCC CVC CCVCC	Silent e VCe
1. One (1) vowel, followed by	1. One (1) vowel, followed by
2. One (1) or more consonants	2. One (1) consonant and a final "e"
3. The short sound for the vowel	3. The long sound for the vowel

4. Display a syllable (e.g., **sun**). Ask students to decide which syllable pattern it follows. Encourage students to refer to the syllable pattern rule cards to help.

sun

5. Repeat the process with a syllable representing the other syllable type for the sort (e.g., **cake**).

> cake

6. Have students place syllables that are the same type under the rule card or in a column in a pocket chart or tacked to a bulletin board.

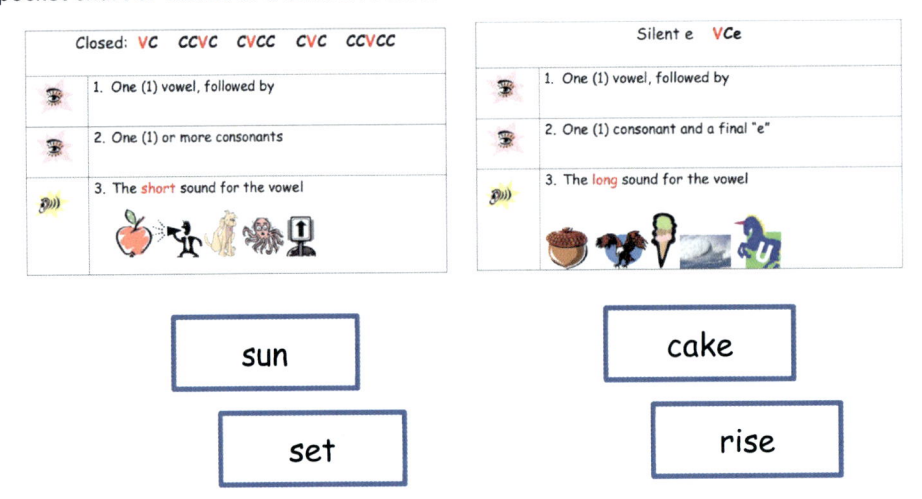

Closed: VC CCVC CVCC CVC CCVCC
1. One (1) vowel, followed by
2. One (1) or more consonants
3. The short sound for the vowel

Silent e VCe
1. One (1) vowel, followed by
2. One (1) consonant and a final "e"
3. The long sound for the vowel

> sun   cake
> set   rise

7. Practice with the remainder of the syllables in the pre-planned list until all of the syllables prepared for the sort have been placed in a category.

8. Have students read the syllables in each category emphasizing the vowel sound for that type of syllable (e.g., short for Closed syllables; long for Silent **e** syllables). If students sort any of the syllables incorrectly, they may self-correct when reading the syllables within the category.

9. If the preplanned syllables are part of multi-syllable words, end the sort by building those longer words. This can be done in two ways:

    a. Dictate a multi-syllable word (e.g., **inflate**). Have students find the syllables that make up the longer word (e.g., **in** + **flate**).

    b. Have students find syllable pairs that can be put together for form a longer word (e.g., **cup** + **cake** to make **cupcake**) on their own.

The first approach provides more structure for the students. The second approach is more difficult and is better used when students have gained proficiency with guided word building at the syllable level.

Tips for Teaching

[1]To show the relationship of syllables to longer words, select syllables for the sort that can be combined to form a multi-syllable word. For example, the single-syllable words (syllables): **in, sun, set, cup, cake, rise, side** can be combined to build the two-syllable words **sunset, cupcake, sunrise,** and **inside**.

[2]Another source of syllables for sorts are from decodable and authentic text that the students are reading.

Syllable Pattern Identification: Syllable Sort (Stage 2)

Objective: To practice vowel pattern (syllable types) categorization

Target students: 2 – 3

Materials needed: Pre-planned syllables for at least two syllable types that the students have learned[1]; rule cards for syllable types that are targeted for the sort

How to do activity:

Follow these basic steps to guide students through the sorting process:

1. Tell students that they are going to sort syllables to practice inspecting the vowel and the consonant(s) that may come after the vowel. Tell them that the syllables that they are going to sort (e.g., **plan, et, or, bit, Ve, nus, ex, plore, tel, e, scope, Nep, tune**) are parts of words that they will need to pronounce correctly to read *Explore Our Solar System*[2] (e.g., **planet, orbit, Venus, explore, telescope, Neptune**).

2. Review the syllable pattern rule cards, the vowel sounds associated with them (e.g., short, long, r-controlled), and related Syllable Stories that correspond to the types of syllables that are the focus of the sort (e.g., Closed, Open, Silent **e**, and R-controlled). (See **Syllable Inspector** page 84 for more information about each syllable type.)

3. Display a syllable (e.g., **or**). Ask students to decide which syllable pattern it follows (R-Controlled). Encourage students to refer to the syllable pattern rule cards to help. Place the syllable below the correct syllable pattern rule care.

   or

4. Repeat the process with a syllable representing each of the other syllable types for the sort (e.g., **bit, tune, Ve**).

| bit | Ve | or | tune |

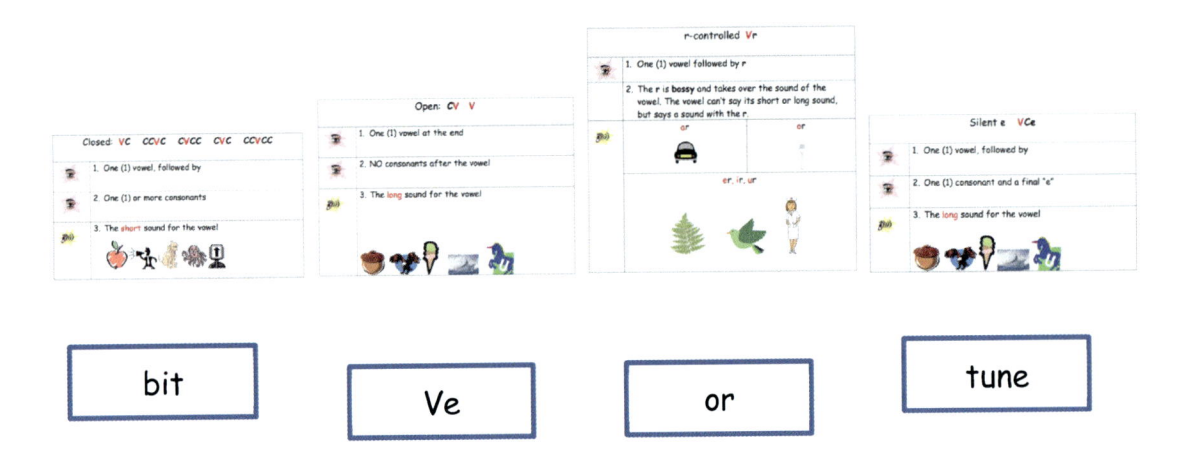

5. Practice with the remainder of the syllables in the pre-planned list until all of the syllables prepared for the sort have been placed in a category.

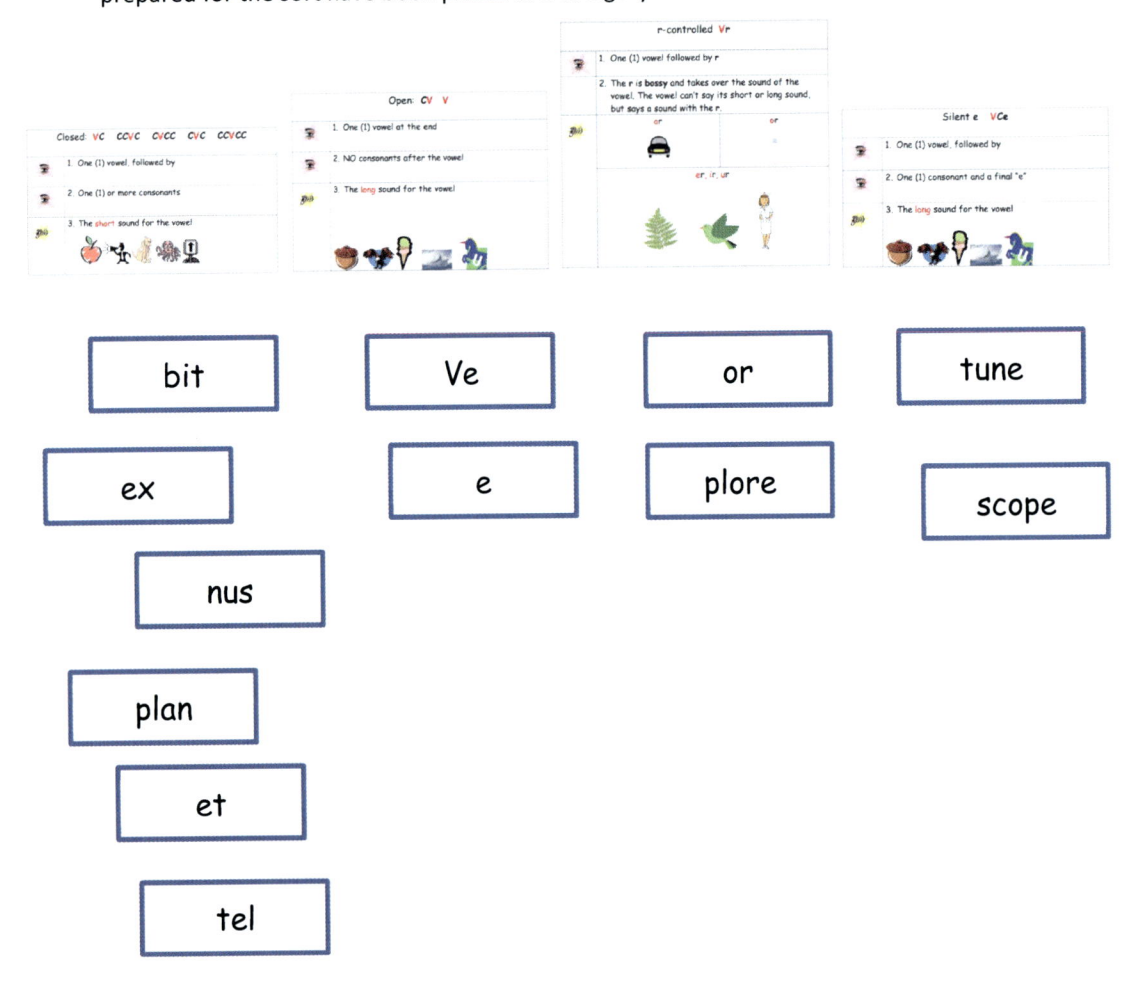

bit	Ve	or	tune
ex	e	plore	scope
nus			
plan			
et			
tel			

6. Have students read the syllables in each category emphasizing the vowel sound for that type of syllable (e.g., short for Closed syllables; long for Silent e syllables). If students sort any of the syllables incorrectly, reading the syllables within the category often helps them self-correct the pronunciation.

7. End the activity by having students build the words that are from the text selection. This can be done in two ways:
    a. Dictate a word from the targeted list (e.g., **orbit**). Have students find the syllables that make up the longer word (e.g., **or** + **bit**).
    b. Have students find syllable pairs that can be put together for form a longer word (e.g., **ex** + **plore** to make **explore**) on their own.

The first approach provides more structure for the students. The second approach is more difficult and is better used when students have gained proficiency with guided word building at the syllable level.

During this step, help students adjust pronunciation due to stress patterns. For example, the syllables **tel** + **e** + **scope** are pronounced / t ĕ l / / ē / / s k ō p /. However, if pronounced together as a word, the long **e** in the middle syllable doesn't sound right; it should be reduced to schwa sounding more like short **u**. With practice, stress patterns become more familiar to students but using the full vowel equivalent—that is short or long sounds—helps them get to a close approximation of the pronunciation.

Tips for Teaching

[1]To show the relationship of syllables to longer words, select syllables for the sort that can be combined to form words from text selections. This is particularly helpful to develop the pronunciation and recognition of vocabulary in content areas. For example, the syllables **plan, et, or, bit, Ve, nus, ex, plore, tel, e, scope, Nep,** and **tune** can be combined to build the two-syllable words **planet, orbit, Venus, explore, telescope, Neptune** for an informational selection on the solar system.

[2]The text selection *Explore Our Solar System* can be found at www.readworks.org.

Syllable Pattern Identification: *Schwa*llowed Vowels (Stage 2)

Objective: To identify accent (stressed), unaccented (unstressed) syllables and schwa in multi-syllable words

Target students: 2 – 3

Materials needed: Pre-planned word list, vowel posters, Schwa card[1] (i.e., what do you see; what do you hear)

How to do activity:

1. Review the vowels sounds (e.g., short and long) using the vowel posters. Have students place one of their hands under their chins to feel their chins drop and touch their hands each time they say a vowel sound.

2. Say each of the following words; have students repeat them while continuing to place one hand under their chins: **dog**, **bas**ket, **in**terest, **sing**ing, **bench**, *a*lone, *e*scape, **Sat**urday, **pen**cil, re**turn**. After each word, ask students to tell how many times their chins touched their hands.

3. Repeat the list of words: **dog**, **bas**ket, **in**terest, **sing**ing, **bench**, *a*lone, *e*scape, **Sat**urday, **pen**cil, re**turn**. This time, point out to students that their mouths open the farthest (i.e., their chins drop the most) for the accented syllables. Ask students to identify the accented syllable, represented in bold font.

4. Display the Schwa card. Explain that sometimes we see one of the vowel sounds, but it doesn't sound as is usually does. Illustrate this by writing the word **basket** on a white board or chart paper. While placing your hand under your chin, say **basket** for the students exaggerating the stressed syllable (**bas**). Have students identify the vowel they see (**a**) and the sound they hear (short / ă /). Continue with the second syllable (**ket**). Have students identify the vowel they see (**e**) and the sound they hear (short / ĭ /). Tell students that the vowel in **ket** is the schwa. It is in the unaccented (i.e., unstressed) syllable.

5. Repeat this process with the other words on the list. For each word:
    a. Write the word on the white board or chart paper
    b. Say the word using the hand under the chin to determine the accented and unaccented syllables
    c. Ask students to focus on the vowel they see and the sound they hear
    d. When the vowel in a syllable is reduced to schwa—that is it isn't long or short—tell students this is a "*schwa*llowed" vowel.

Tips for Teaching

[1]Initial instruction in schwa focuses on identification of accented and unaccented syllables and the reduced vowel sound, which we refer to as schwa. The guidelines—that is the various conditions when schwa most often occurs—can be explained gradually as students encounter these patterns.

Phonetically Irregular Words

The following activity focuses on reading phonetically irregular words accurately and automatically.

Domain: Phonics

Background information for this activity:

The majority of words in English—nearly 85%, in fact—are spelled according to phonetically predictable sound-to-letter correspondences. Unfortunately, there are a small number of frequently used words that do not follow these predictable correspondences. They are rule breakers; something about the relationship between their pronunciation and spelling don't match. Rule breaker words must be taught explicitly, pointing out the part that breaks the rules, and practiced as a distinct group of words until they are recognized on sight (i.e., automatically and accurately). For example, to teach the word **said**, which is pronounced / s ĕ d /, instruction needs to point out that the letters **ai** are pronounce / ĕ / rather than / ā /--breaking the rule for the predictable sound-spelling correspondence (i.e., **ai** usually represents / ā /.

The following table displays this activity for Stages 1 and 2. The activity is the same for both stages. Critical to the activity's success is careful attention to gradual and cumulative presentation of phonetically irregular words.

Stage 0	Stage 1	Stage 2
	Rule Breaker Words (Read phonetically irregular words)	Rule Breaker Words (Read phonetically irregular words)

Phonetically Irregular Words: Rule Breakers...Beware! (Stages 1 and 2)

Objective: To read phonetically irregular words accurately and automatically[1]

Target students: K - 3

Materials needed: Preplanned word lists with phonetically irregular words[2], formatted tables[3] (2 x 2, 4 x 4, 6 x 6)

How to do activity:

Phase 1: How to teach a rule breaker word

1. Explain to students that they are going to practice reading rule breaker words. These words may have some letters that "play fair" and are pronounced using what they know about the sounds to say for the letters. But there is at least one letter in each word that breaks the rules.
2. Write the word **said** on the white board or chart paper to illustrate what a rule breaker word is.
3. Say the word for the students (/ s ĕ d /). Point out that the **ai** is pronounced with the short **e** (i.e., / ĕ /), not long a (/ ā /), "breaking the rules" about what they know about letter-sound associations.
4. Model saying the word again (/ s ĕ d /). Next, name the letters in the word (**s – a – i – d**). Finally, repeat the whole word (/ s ĕ d /).
5. Have students repeat the same steps.
6. Repeat the explanation with another word. Write **from** on the white board or chart paper. Say the word for the students (/ f r ŭ m /). Ask students to identify the rule-breaking letter (**o**) and tell what sound it is saying (/ ŭ /). Point out that the **o** is pronounced as short **u** (/ ŭ /), not short **o**, breaking the rule.
7. Continue to practice the rule breaker words on flash cards or in the formatted tables described in Phase 2 of this activity. The goal is to recognize these high frequency, rule-breaking words "on sight."

Phase 2: Focus on automatic recognition of rule breaker words

1. Provide students with a table of words that has been formatted based on the rule breaker words they have learned. Explain that they will practice reading Rule Breaker words.
2. Read the first row and point to each word while reading the word. Point out the rule breaker part of each word. Have students highlight or underline the irregular part of each word in the first row.

though	friend	would	been
been	would	though	friend

3. Reread the first row with the students.
4. Next, ask each student to read the first row of words and provide corrective feedback. For example, if a student reads the word **said** as (/ s ā d /, i.e., with a long a sound), point out that the **ai** is pronounced with the short **e** (/ ĕ /) sound. These letters are rule breakers in this word.
5. When students have accurately and independently read each word in the first row, have them read each successive row to build automaticity.
8. Practice the same Rule Breaker word tables on subsequent days to ensure automatic recognition.

Tips for Teaching

[1]Note: Accurately and automatically = word is read ≤ 3 seconds without a mistake

[2]Appendix pages 144 and 145 provides a list of phonetically irregular words and a list of the first 100 high frequency words. Teachers can select and gradually teach the words on this list in a systematic and cumulative way. They can also choose words from the list that appear in the text selection that students are reading to ensure that students can recognize them accurately and fluently **before** reading the text.

[3]The format of the grid (2 x 2, 4 x 4, or 6 x 6) makes it possible to adjust the task to the difficulty level that matches the student's reading level. The number of rule breaker words practiced at any time controls for the difficulty level of the task. The purpose of the grid is to practice the same words in a rearranged sequence to build automatic recognition.

Examples of these levels are illustrated below:

Level 1: 2 x 2 Table

of	from
from	of

Level 2: 4 x 4 Table

though	friend	would	been
been	would	though	friend
friend	though	been	would
would	been	friend	though

Level 3: 6 x 6 Table

answer	should	learn	often	enough	thought
thought	often	answer	learn	should	enough
often	answer	thought	enough	learn	should
should	learn	often	thought	answer	often
learn	enough	should	answer	often	learn
enough	though	enough	should	thought	answer

Automatic Word Recognition

The following activities target the development of automatic and fluent word recognition.

Domain: Phonics

Background information for this activity:

Accurate and automatic recognition of words is necessary in order to devote working memory to comprehension, rather than to decoding, that is figuring out the words. While speed (rate) is important, reading groups of words with expression (i.e., as the reader would speak the words) is equally important.

Fluent reading—that is accurate and automatic word recognition—is an essential step in developing reading proficiency. One aspect of fluent reading has to do with rate (i.e., speed), usually referred to as correct words per minute (CWPM). Evidence suggests that achieving targeted fluency rates[1] contributes to reading comprehension. Another aspect of fluent reading has to do with prosody (i.e., inflection and intonation of word and phrase pronunciation). Reading with prosody (i.e., in phrases) suggests that the reader has incorporated a layer of understanding of the words, phrases, and sentences, which also contributes to comprehension.

The following table displays these activities for Stages 1 and 2. The activities are the same for both stages. Words used for this activity should be taught gradually and cumulatively prior to their use in these activities to ensure that students know them and can then focus on automatic recognition.

Stage 0	Stage 1	Stage 2
	Fluent Reading (Read words in phrases with prosody) Beat the Clock (Read words and phrases accurately and automatically)	Fluent Reading (Read words in phrases with prosody) Beat the Clock (Read words and phrases accurately and automatically)

[1] See page 149 for updated ORF norms

Automatic Word Recognition: Fluent Reading (Stages 1 and 2)

Objective: To read words and phrases fluently (accurately and automatically) [1]

Target students: K - 3

Materials needed: Copies of a preselected list of words and phrases from a decodable text. Words are written or typed on the left-hand side of the page and phrases on the right. The paper is then folded in half.

How to do activity:

1. Distribute a word/phrase list to each student in a small group (4 – 6 students)
2. Begin by placing the folded paper with the word list face up in front of each student.

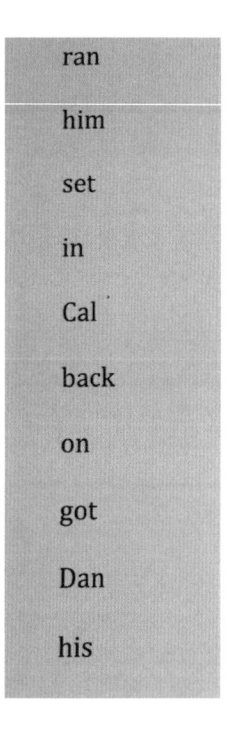

ran
him
set
in
Cal
back
on
got
Dan
his

3. Point to each word and read the list of words as each student points and follows along.
4. Next, have the students read the list of words, accurately and automatically. Provide corrective feedback if necessary.
5. Next, unfold the paper to reveal the phrases and ask if students notice anything about these phrases.

ran	ran up
him	to him
set	set up camp
in	in back
Cal	of Cal's house
back	go back
on	on Cal's lap
got	got in the tent
Dan	Dan and Tramp
his	his dog Tramp

6. Read each phrase while scooping it to demonstrate prosodic reading.
7. The teacher scaffolds as the students read the list of words offering corrective feedback as needed.
8. The teacher may choose to have the students reread the list of words several times to gain automaticity.

Tips for Teaching

[1]After students achieve the targeted fluency rate with individual (isolated) words, use the same words to build phrases to practice for automaticity and prosody.

Automatic Word Recognition: Beat the Clock (Stages 1 and 2)

Objective: To read words, phrases, and sentences[1] fluently (accurately and automatically)

Target students: K – 3

Materials needed: Copies of preselected fluency word table[2] of words, phrases and sentences from text material; stopwatches or times, graph paper or fluency graph[3] for recording scores

How to do activity:

1. Pair students with a peer partner. Provide each student with a fluency table and a fluency graph.
2. Demonstrate how you use the stopwatch[4] to time the number of words the students read in one minute while marking the words read incorrectly on the fluency table. Explain how to calculate the score—that is the number of correct words read in a minute—using the numbers in the right column of the fluency table.
3. Model the process with one of the students to illustrate timing, marking words and calculating the score.
4. Have peer partners take turns reading the words in the fluency table to each other while being timed. Observe each pair and give feedback about how they are marking words for their partners.
5. Have each student read the fluency table of words twice, alternating turns. Have them record the number of words for each trial in the space provided at the bottom of the fluency word table.
6. Complete the activity by having students record the date, selection, and their best scores from the two trials on the fluency graph.

Tips for Teaching

[1]Begin this activity using words. Once students are familiar with the routine and become proficient at timing their partner and marking errors, students can also practice reading phrases and sentences.

[2]Select the words for this activity from the decodable (Stage 1) or authentic (Stage 2) text that students are reading. Fill in the Fluency Table (See Appendix 146 for a blank table) with one word per cell of the first row. Then, randomly repeat the words in successive rows, keeping the frequency of each word as consistent as possible. The sample below illustrates words with vowel teams (Talkers and Whiners) from the selection *How Do Seeds Grow?*.

Fluency Word Table

seed	grow	soon	out	break	root	down	shoot	leave	how	10
grow	seed	out	soon	root	break	leave	down	how	shoot	20
break	out	soon	seed	grow	down	root	how	shoot	leave	30
leave	shoot	down	break	soon	seed	grow	out	root	how	40
shoot	how	leave	root	down	out	soon	seed	break	grow	50
how	leave	root	down	out	soon	break	shoot	grow	seed	60
down	root	break	shoot	how	leave	out	grow	seed	soon	70
leave	break	how	leave	down	grow	seed	soon	out	root	80
out	down	seed	grow	seed	shoot	leave	root	soon	break	90
root	soon	grow	how	shoot	leave	shoot	break	down	out	100

1st Trial _____   2nd Trial _____

[3]Each student will have a fluency graph (see Appendix 147 for a blank graph) with a place for the date and title of the text selection from which the words are chosen. The graph serves as a record of students' fluency practice (i.e., CWPM) throughout the year.

Correct Words Per Minute										
170										
160										
150										
140										
130										
120										
110										
100										
90										
80										
70										
60										
50										
40										
35										
20										
10										
Title										
Date										

See Appendix 148 for norms table for fluency rates

[4]As students become proficient in the procedure individuals can take turns using the stopwatch to be the timer for the class.

Text Selection Skills Analyses

Any text selection provides opportunities for teachers to help students apply content, skills and strategies. In the case of the phonics domain, text provides the context for students to apply their phoneme-grapheme knowledge.

To take advantage of these opportunities, teachers must first consider what students have *already* learned through direct and explicit instruction. This surface level learning is a prerequisite in order for students to transfer this learning to text (Fisher, Frey & Hattie, 2016). Next teachers need to analyze text to determine what opportunities exist for students to practice and apply content, skills and strategies acquired through direct instruction. This requires that teachers preview the text to identify the domain-specific content (e.g., phonics) that can be reinforced when reading the text selection. The use of text selections requires consideration of what students have been taught previously and what they have learned, as well as the skill requirements needed to read the selection. This analytical process is called cognitive preparation during which teachers must consider the match between what students know (i.e., content, skills and strategies) and the demands of the task (e.g., phonics) so their students can access and master the meaning of the text.

In this section of *Phonics: Knowledge to Practice*, we model this process with a series of different texts. For each text selection, we provide a **Text Analysis** table with examples of domain-specific learning objectives that are applicable for the selection. The table provides learning objectives for multiple domains to illustrate the range of options in using a text selection. The table of objectives also demonstrates that it is possible to integrate several aspects of literacy development through strategic use of the same text selection. Following the objectives, we draw from activities in the **Activities for Instruction and Informal Assessment** section to show how to tailor the activities to the text selection. The **Activity Application to Text** table includes a "Think Aloud" component in which we offer an example of the thinking that should occur to make a match between what students know and what the text offers for skill application to foster the alphabetic principle and orthographic awareness. The **Text Analysis** examples are presented in the order of the activities on page 60 not according to Stages 0 to 2.

Stage 0

The Hungry Girl[1]

"I'm hungry!"
Said the little girl
To her dearest dad
"Would you like to sip some soup?
That's what your brother had."

"No! I'm hungry!"
Said the little girl
To her dearest dad
"Would you like to taste this toast?
That's what your brother had."

"No! I'm hungry!"
Said the little girl
To her dearest dad
"Would you like to munch a muffin?
That's what your brother had."

No! I'm hungry!"
Said the little girl
To her dearest dad
"Would you like some yummy yogurt?
That's not what your brother had."

"Yes I would!"
Said the little girl
To her dearest dad
She ate the yogurt by herself,
Which made her brother mad!

Text Analysis

Alphabetic Principle	Vocabulary/Syntax	Comprehension
<ul><li>Establish one-to-one relationship between words in print and spoken words</li><li>Letter knowledge: Recognize and name letters</li><li>Phonological Awareness: Initial phoneme isolation and identification using alliterative words (sip, some, soup; taste, toast; munch, muffin; yummy, yogurt)</li></ul>	<ul><li>Discuss words from the poem that may be unfamiliar (sip, munch, yummy)</li><li>Read in meaningful grammatical phrases</li></ul>	Ask literal and inferential questions

Phonemic Awareness and Phonics: Knowledge to Practice   113

Activity Application to Text

Activity Selection "Think Aloud"	Lesson Focus: Phonics – Awareness of alphabetic principle in connected text
	Activity: Synchronized Reading (See page 63)
	Group size: Small Group

The repetitive pattern in the poem *The Hungry Girl* is easy for students to memorize. This feature makes this poem a natural choice for the activity **Synchronized Reading**. As students point to each word as they read, they increase awareness of the sound-to-letter match. The alliterative strings of words (**s**ip **s**ome **s**oup, **m**unch **m**uffin, **t**aste – **t**oast, and **y**ummy **y**ogurt) provide additional support to help students achieve the alphabetic principle.	Materials needed: The Hungry Girl written on poster paper or displayed on Smartboard, a pointer, copies of text for students' use
	
	How to do activity:
	1. Project or post the text for all students to see.
	2. On the first reading, ask students to listen to the poem as you recite it slowly and with prosody. Point to each word as you read. Emphasize the following in one of the recitations:
	   - Reading from the top of the page to the bottom
	   - Reading words from left to right
	   - Return sweep at the end of each row.
	   - Some words (e.g., hungry, dearest, brother) get two taps because they have two parts (i.e., syllables)
	3. During the second reading of the poem, stop intermittently to explain that the word you are pointing to begins with a sound that corresponds to the letter (e.g., the word soup begins with the / s / sound and it has the letter **s** at the beginning of the word). Teach the same concept with an ending continuant sound (e.g., the word muffin ends with the / n / sound and it has the letter **n** at the end of the word).
	4. Provide students with a copy of the text at their seat/table. Recite the poem several more times and ask students to point to the words on their copy as you read.
	5. Finally, ask individual children to "read" the poem in front of the class with the pointer. Guide each child through the process, pointing out the match between what their mouth is saying and the sounds that the letter they are pointing to represents.

[1] Go to www.ReadWorks.com for a printable version of *The Hungry Girl*

Stage 2

How Do Seeds Grow?[2]

Many plants start out as small seeds. How does a seed grow?

First, it falls or is put into dirt. The sun's light helps the seed to grow. The seed gets energy from water.

Before long, the seed breaks open. Roots start to grow down into the dirt. Then a shoot pushes up through the dirt. The stem and leaves pop out next.

Soon, the little plant will be grown-up.

Text Analysis

Decoding/Encoding	Vocabulary/Syntax	Comprehension
• Develop phoneme-grapheme associations • Develop knowledge of syllable types • Practice distinguishing and reading different syllable types	• Multiple meaning words (e.g., plant, fall, leaves)	• Identify sequence of events; use transition words that signal sequence

Activity Application to Text

Activity Selection "Think Aloud"	Lesson Focus: Phonics – Encoding to decoding
	Activity: Sound-letter maps (See page 69)
	Group Size: Small Group

The code-emphasis text selection *How Do Seeds Grow?* is an excellent source of words to use for the activity **Sound-Letter Maps**. This activity fosters students' understanding of the speech-to-print match, particularly for the long vowel sounds that have several different spellings (e.g., long / ō / spelled **o** as in **open** and **ow** as in **grow**).	Materials needed:
	Phoneme-Grapheme Map or graph paper with numbered rows, tokens; list of words from the text (**seed, stem, help, next, start, grow, first, root**)
	
	How to do activity:
	1. Provide each student with a Phoneme-Grapheme Map, tokens, and a pencil. Model the procedure as follows.
	   a. First, identify the number of sounds in a word:
	      i. Say a word on the list (e.g., **seed**)
	      ii. Place one token per sound on the Phoneme-Grapheme Map (i.e., move one token for / s /, another for / ē /, another for / d /. Identify the number of sounds in the word (3)
	      iii. Point to each token and say the sound that corresponds from the word (/ s / / ē / / d / and repeat the word (**seed**)
	   b. Next, replace the token by writing the grapheme to represent each sound in the corresponding box. Name each letter aloud as you write it.
	      i. Ask students: What sound do you hear? (/ s /)
	      ii. Then ask: What letter(s) do you write? (**s**)
	      iii. Ask students: What sound do you hear? (/ ē /)
	      iv. Then ask: What letter(s) do you write? (**ee**)

	v. Ask students: What sound do you hear? (/ *d*/)
	vi. Then ask: What letter(s) do you write? (**d**)
	c. Continue with other words on the list. Check that students are pronouncing the word correctly and synchronizing saying the sounds as they name and write each letter. Provide additional modeling of the task and immediate corrective feedback.
	d. Finally, have students write the letters for the word on the line to the right of the boxes to form the word. Be sure to have students read the whole word after they write it. At the end, have students read the column of words to practice reading the words they just mapped.

[2] Go to www.ReadWorks.com for a printable version of *How Do Seeds Grow?*

Stage 1

Cal and Tramp Camp[3]

Cal said, "Let's camp."
His dog Tramp ran up to him.
Dan and Tramp set up camp.
They put up a tent in back of Cal's house.
Cal and Tramp got in the tent.
Then they heard "HOOT! HOOT!"
Tramp jumped on Cal's lap.
"That was just an owl," Dan said.
No one slept.
"Let's go back in the house!"
Tramp ran fast!

Text Analysis

Decoding/Encoding	Vocabulary/Syntax	Comprehension
• Develop phoneme-grapheme associations • Develop accurate and automatic word recognition using phonics knowledge	• Grammar: past tense verbs (regular and irregular; e.g., jumped, slept, ran, heard)	• Identify the sequence of events in the story (i.e., identify plot)

Activity Application to Text

Activity Selection "Think Aloud"	Lesson Focus: Phonics – Encoding to decoding
	Activity: Build and Blend (See page 80)
	Group Size: Small Group
The decodable text selection *Cal and Tramp Camp* is a rich source of words composed of transparent (i.e., one-to-one) sound-to-letter correspondences. These words can be used in the activity **Build and Blend** to provide practice in blending phonemes together to read words.	Materials needed: List of words (**Cal, up, him, tent, back, got, in, lap, slept, fast**); Large cards (5 x 7 or 8 ½ x 11) with lower case letter(s) including single consonants, single vowels needed to build the words on the preplanned list (**c, a, i, u, p, h, l, m, t, e, n, b, k, g, o, s, f**) How to do activity: 1. Distribute the letter cards—one per student—according to the words on the preplanned word list. 2. Have the students take turns saying the name and sound for their letters. If a child has difficulty remembering the sound, prompt with its key word (e.g., itch for / ĭ /). 3. Say a word from the preplanned list (e.g., **him**). Have students identify the sounds in the word (e.g., / h / / ĭ / / m /). 4. Ask students who have the letters that represent these sounds to come to the front of the class and build the word (e.g., **h – i – m**). Use the cue "Build It." 5. Stand behind the students with the letters. Tap each letter-holder on the head as they say the sound their letter makes (e.g., / h / / ĭ / / m /). Say "Blend It" to have the students combine the sounds to say the word (e.g., him). Have students hold hands or link arms as they blend the sounds together and say the word. 6. Repeat with the next word on the preplanned list of words utilizing the letters that the students have for building.

Stage 2

How Do Seeds Grow?[4]

Many plants start out as small seeds. How does a seed grow?

First, it falls or is put into dirt. The sun's light helps the seed to grow. The seed gets energy from water.

Before long, the seed breaks open. Roots start to grow down into the dirt. Then a shoot pushes up through the dirt. The stem and leaves pop out next.

Soon, the little plant will be grown-up.

Text Analysis

Decoding/Encoding	Vocabulary/Syntax	Comprehension
• Develop phoneme-grapheme associations • Develop knowledge of syllable types • Practice distinguishing and reading different syllable types	• Multiple meaning words (e.g., **plant, fall, leaves**)	• Identify sequence of events; use transition words that signal sequence

Activity Application to Text

Activity Selection "Think Aloud"	Lesson Focus: Phonics – automatic word reading
	Activity: Syllable Sort (See page 97)
	Group Size: Small Group
The informational text *How Do Seeds Grow?* includes a high percentage of decodable words representing most of the six syllable types. The activity **Syllable Sort** gives students an opportunity to classify words from this text selection based on the different vowel patterns (i.e., the six syllable types). This practice promotes accuracy and automaticity when reading these patterns in connected text.	Materials needed: Vowel posters and rule cards for the following syllable types: Closed, Open, Silent B, Vowel Teams (Talkers and Whiners) and R-Controlled; the following words written on index cards for sorting: Single syllable: **plants, start, out, seeds, how, grow, first, dirt, helps, gets, roots, down, then, shoot, up, stem, leaves, pop, out, next, soon, will** Multi-syllable: **lit tle, en er gy, o pen** How to do activity: 1. Tell students that they are going to sort syllables to practice inspecting the vowel and the consonant(s) that may come after the vowel. Being able to do this helps them read and spell words. 2. Review the vowels sounds (e.g., short, long, and r-controlled) that are the focus of the targeted syllable patterns for the lesson. 3. Review the syllable pattern rule cards and related Syllable Stories that correspond to the types of syllables that are the focus of the sort. 4. Display a syllable (e.g., **plants**). Ask students to decide which syllable pattern it follows. Encourage students to refer to the syllable pattern rule cards to help. (Closed) 5. Repeat the process with a syllable representing another syllable type for the sort (e.g., **seeds**). (Vowel Team – Talkers)

	6. Have students place syllables that are the same type under the rule card, which is in a column in a pocket chart or tacked to a bulletin board.
	7. Practice with the remainder of the words in the pre-planned word list until all of the words for the sort are placed in a category.
	8. End the activity by having students read the sorted columns of words and syllables. Review the syllable rule cards as needed.
	9. End the sort by having the student first build and then sort the syllables in the multi-syllable words little, open, and energy.
	10. Have students read the syllables in each category emphasizing the vowel sound for that type of syllable (e.g., short for Closed syllables; long for Silent **e** syllables). If students sort any of the syllables incorrectly, they may self-correct when reading the syllables within the category.

[4] Go to www.ReadWorks.com for a printable version of *How Do Seeds Grow?*

Stage 2

Magic Tomatoes[5]

Luke's father is a farmer. To be more precise, his dad is a fruit-and-vegetable farmer. Instead of cows, pigs, sheep, and horses, corn, squash, lettuce, and tomatoes surround Luke's house.

Luke does not mind that there are not any animals. In fact, he likes living on a fruit-and-vegetable farm much better. If you asked Luke, he would say that a fruit-and-vegetable farm is magical.

"What do you mean, magical?" Luke's friend Tom asked one day.

"Well, it's like this," said Luke. "My dad casts a spell, and soon enough the fruits and vegetables appear where there used to be bare dirt!"

Now, Luke knows that this is not really magic. But all the same, he feels it is pretty special that his dad is able to create something as grand as a cornfield where there used to be nothing. Sometimes, Luke sets his alarm clock, so he can wake up before the sunrise, too. He eats cereal with his dad and asks him what spells he is going to cast.

"I'm planting tomatoes today, son," Luke's father explained. "Tomatoes ripen best in very hot summer heat, so I need to plant the seeds early in spring. That way there will be tall, healthy tomato vines once August arrives."

Text Analysis

Decoding/Encoding	Vocabulary/Syntax	Comprehension
• Read words with unaccented syllables containing the schwa • Increase reading rate • Read phonetically irregular words	• Morphology lesson with change in parts of speech (e.g., magic/magical; attend/attention; farm/farmer)	• Identify elements of a story (i.e., setting, characters, plot)

Activity Application to Text

Activity Selection "Think Aloud"	Lesson Focus: Phonics – accent and schwa
	Activity: Schwallowed Vowels (See page 102)
	Group Size: Small Group
The narrative text, *Magic Tomatoes*, includes a number of multisyllabic words (i.e., two- and three-syllable words) that can be used to illustrate the schwa sound and to practice reading words with accented and	Materials needed: The following words written on index cards: Luke, alarm, vegetable, surrounded, lettuce, tomatoes, animals, magical, appear, able Vowel posters, Schwa card (i.e., what do you see; what do you hear) How to do activity: 1. Review the vowels sounds (e.g., short and long) using the vowel posters. Have students place one of their hands under their chins to feel their chins drop and touch their hands each time they say a vowel sound.

unaccented syllables.
***Schwa**llowed Vowels* is designed to help students recognize unstressed syllables and that impact on the sound the vowels represent.
	2. Say each of the following words; have students repeat them while continuing to place one hand under their chins: **Luke**, *a*l**arm**, **veg**e*ta*ble, su*r***round**ed, **let**tuce, to**ma**toes, **an**i*mals*, **mag**i*cal*, a**ppear**, **a**ble
	After each word, ask students to tell how many times their chins touched their hands.
	3. Repeat the list of words: **Luke**, *a*l**arm**, **veg**e*ta*ble, su*r***round**ed, **let**tuce, to**ma**toes, **an**i*mals*, **mag**i*cal*, a**ppear**, **a**ble
	4. This time, point out to students that their mouths open the farthest (i.e., their chins drop the most) for the accented syllables. Ask students to identify the accented syllable, represented in bold font.
	5. Display the Schwa card. Explain that sometimes we see one of the vowel sounds, but it doesn't sound as is usually does. Illustrate this by writing the word alarm on a white board or chart paper. While placing your hand under your chin, say alarm for the students exaggerating the stressed syllable (l**arm**). Have students identify the vowel they see (ar) and the sound they hear (/ ar /). Show the other syllable (a). Have students identify the vowel they see (a) and the sound they hear (short / ŭ /). Tell students that the vowel in the syllable a is the schwa. It is in the unaccented (i.e., unstressed) syllable.
	6. Repeat this process with the other words on the list. For each word:
	   a. Write the word on the white board or chart paper
	   b. Say the word using the hand under the chin to determine the accented and unaccented syllables
	   c. Ask students to focus on the vowel they **see** and the sound they **hear**
	   d. When a syllable has a vowel reduced to schwa, point this out to students. Tell students this is a *schwa*llowed vowel.

Activity Selection "Think Aloud"	Lesson Focus: Phonics – accent and schwa
	Activity: Rule Breakers…Beware! (See page 104)
	Group Size: Small Group
As with most text in Stage 2, the narrative text, *Magic Tomatoes*, utilizes a number of phonetically irregular words. To increase students' sight recognition of these words in context, the activity **Rule Breakers…Beware!** provides explicit practice with some of these high frequency words prior to reading the selection.	Materials needed: The following words used to fill in a 6 x 6 table (See page 106): does, would, enough, what, pretty, once Vowel posters, Schwa card (i.e., what do you see; what do you hear) How to do activity: 1. Explain to students that they are going to practice reading Rule Breakers. These words may have some letters that 'play fair' and are pronounced using what they know about the sounds to say for the letters. But there is at least one letter in each word that breaks the rules. 2. Write the word does on the white board or chart paper to illustrate what a Rule Breaker word is. Say the word for the students (/ d ŭ z /). Point out that the **oe** is pronounced with the short u, not long o and that the **s** is pronounce with the / z / sound…breaking the rules.

	3. Provide students with a table of with the words from the selection and explain that they will practice reading Rule Breaker words for the story they are going to read.
	4. Read the first row and point to each word while reading the word. Point out the rule breaker part of each word. Have students highlight or underline the irregular part of each word in the first row.
	5. Reread the first row with the students.
	6. Next, ask each student to read the first row of words and provide corrective feedback. For example, if a student reads the word **does** as (/ d ō s /, i.e., with a long o sound and / s / for the final letter), point out that the **oe** is pronounced with the short u sound and that the **s** is pronounced as / z /. These letters are rule breakers.
	7. When students have accurately and independently read each word in the first row, have them read each successive row to build automaticity.
	8. Practice the same Rule Breaker word tables on subsequent days to ensure automatic recognition.

[5] Go to www.ReadWorks.com for a printable version of *Magic Tomatoes*

Stage 1

Cal and Tramp Camp[3]

Cal said, "Let's camp."
His dog Tramp ran up to him.
Dan and Tramp set up camp.
They put up a tent in back of Cal's house.
Cal and Tramp got in the tent.
Then they heard "HOOT! HOOT!"
Tramp jumped on Cal's lap.
"That was just an owl," Dan said.
No one slept.
"Let's go back in the house!"
Tramp ran fast!

Text Analysis

Decoding/Encoding	Vocabulary/Syntax	Comprehension
• Develop phoneme-grapheme associations • Develop accurate and automatic word recognition using phonics knowledge	• Grammar: past tense verbs (regular and irregular; e.g., jumped, slept, ran, 'set up', heard)	• Identify the sequence of events in the story (i.e., identify plot)

Activity Application to Text

Activity Selection "Think Aloud"	Lesson Focus: Phonics – word and phrase reading
	Activity: Fluent Reading (See page 108)
	Group Size: Small Group
The code-emphasis narrative text, *Cal and Tramp Camp*, contains a high percentage of closed syllable (e.g., **Cal, dog, set**) words, including some with initial and final consonant blends (e.g., **tramp, tent, just**). Using words and phrases from the decodable text, the activity **Fluent Reading** gives students additional practice reading words and phrases with these phonetic features. Such practice fosters accurate and automatic	Materials needed: Copies of the following list of words and phrases from the text selection: Words: ran, set, in, let's, on, got, Dan, then, his, Cal Phrases: ran up, to him, set up camp, in back, of Cal's house, go back, on Cal's lap, got in the tent, Dan and Tramp, his dog Tramp (Appendix page 123) *Cal and Tramp Camp* written on poster paper, white board or Smartboard. How to do activity: 1. Distribute the word/phrase list to each student in a small group (4 – 6 students) 2. Begin by placing the folded paper with the word list face up in front of each student. 3. Point to each word and read the list of words as each student points and follows along. 4. Next, have the students read the list of words, accurately and automatically. Provide corrective feedback if necessary. 5. Next, unfold the paper to reveal the phrases and ask if students notice anything about these phrases. 6. Read each phrase while scooping it to demonstrate prosodic reading, that is reading phrases as you would speak them.

| word reading and prosody, as students read words in phrases. | 7. The teacher scaffolds as the students read the list of words offering corrective feedback as needed, |
| | 8. The teacher may choose to have the students reread the list of words several times to gain automaticity. |

[3] Go to www.ReadWorks.com for a printable version of *Cal and Tramp Camp*

Appendix

Contents for Phonemic Awareness

- Say It and Move It Board
- General sequence for Beginning Phonics Instruction
- Scope and Sequence for Phonetic/Morphemic Elements
- Sample Lesson Design

Contents for Phonics

- The Alphabet Chant (capital letters)
- The Alphabet Chant (lower case letters)
- The Vowel Song
- Cue words for the letters of the alphabet
- Stroke Descriptions for Continuous Manuscript Letters
- Phoneme-Grapheme Map
- Phonetically Irregular Words
- First 100 High Frequency Words
- Fluency Word Table
- Fluency Graph
- Fluency Norms (Hasbrouck)
- Syllable Inspector Cards
    - Closed – VC, CVC, CCVC, CVCC, CCVCC
    - Open – CV, V
    - Silent e - VCe
    - Vowel Teams – VV (Talkers)
    - Vowel Teams – VV (Whiners)
    - R-Controlled – Vr
    - Consonant-le – C-le
    - Schwa
- Sample lesson design
- Sample Words and Phrases for *Cal and Tramp Camp*
- References and Resources

Say It and Move It

[1]From Blachman, B. A., Ball, E. W., Black, R., & Tangel, D. M. (2000). Road to the Code: A Phonological Awareness Program for Young Children. Brookes Publishing: Baltimore, MD

General sequence for Beginning Phonics Instruction
(page 38, 39 LETRS Module 7, second edition)

Phonics Concepts	Examples
Single consonants, high utility	b, s, t, d, m
Short vowels, introduced gradually	/ă/, /ŏ/, /ĭ/, /ŭ/, /ĕ/
Consonant blends (final, initial)	st, -lk, -mp, br, cl
Consonant digraphs	th, wh, sh, ch, ng
Simple endings, such a plurals, -s pronounce /s/ and /z/; past tense –ed, -ing	wishes, wished, wishing
Vowel-consonant-e ("magic e")	late, wide
Odd consonants	qu, x
The "floss" pattern (double f, l, s, at the end of one-syllable word	stuff, mill, grass
Vowel teams	sea, boat, sail
Vowel-r combinations (r-controlled vowels)	for, her car
Derivational suffixes that change part of speech	careful, natural, active
Complex consonant patterns	silent letters, consonant trigraphs that spell a single sound (e.g., -dge, -tch, soft and hard c and g, ck for the /k/ sound, etc.
Multisyllabic words	fantastic, laptop, compete

Scope and Sequence for Phonetic/Morphemic Elements

This chart uses the following labels in the Spelling Stage column: LN (Letter Name), WW (Within Word Pattern), SJ (Syllable Juncture), and DC (Derivational Constancy) from *Word Journeys* by Kathy Ganske.[1]

Phonetic/Morphemic Element	Spelling Stage[1]	Grade Level Reading	Grade Level Spelling
Identifies most common sound for single-letter **Consonants** and **Consonant Digraphs** (*sh, ch, th, wh, ng*)	LN	K	K
Short & Long vowel sounds (*a, e, i, o, u*)	LN	K	K
Closed Syllables (VC, CVC)	LN	K	K
Open Syllables (CV) e.g. we, hi, go, my, ba-by (*y* says long *i* at the end of one-syllable words; *y* usually says long *e* at the end of multi-syllable words)	LN	K (one-syll. words) Gr. 2 (two-syll. words)	K (one-syll. words) Gr. 3 and up (multisyllable words)
Identifies the base word in frequently occurring inflected forms (e.g. look<u>s</u>, look<u>ed</u>, look<u>ing</u>)		K/Gr. 1	
Knows two sounds for the following consonants: *s* may be pronounced /s/ or /z/; *g* may be pronounced /g/ or /j/; *c* may be pronounced /k/ or /s/		Gr. 1	
Understands *y* can function as either a consonant or a vowel: *y* is a consonant when it begins a word or syllable (*yoyo*); final *y* is a vowel (*fly, candy*); *y* may be part of a vowel team (*stay, boy, key*) (sometimes *y* acts as a suffix e.g. dirty)		Gr. 1 (one-syllable words) Gr. 2 (final *y* in two-syllable words)	Gr. 1 (consonantal *y*, final *y* in one-syllable word, *ay*)

Phonetic/Morphemic Element	Spelling Stage[1]	Grade Level Reading	Grade Level Spelling
FLS Rule (*-ff, -ll, -ss, -zz*) e.g. puff, hill, mess, jazz	LN	Gr. 1	Gr. 1
Consonant Digraphs (*sh, ch, th, wh, ck, ng, ph*) (CCVC, CVCC)	LN	Gr. 1 (except *ph* – Gr. 2)	Gr. 1 (except *ph*)
Initial Consonant Blends (CCVC)	LN	Gr. 1	Gr. 1

128

Phonetic/Morphemic Element	Spelling Stage[1]	Grade Level Reading	Grade Level Spelling
Final **Consonant Blends** (CVCC)	LN	Gr. 1	Gr. 1
Closed Syllable Exceptions -*ild* (wild), -*old* (told), -*ind* (find), -*ost* (most), -*olt* (colt)	WW	Gr. 2	Gr. 2
Silent *e* Syllables (VCe) e.g. game, bike, rope, cube	WW	Gr. 1 (may introduce in K)	Gr. 2
Vowel Teams[2]			
• Long *a* – *ai* (rain), *ay* (pay), *eigh* (eight), *ei* (vein)	WW	Gr. 1 *ai, ay* Gr. 2 *ei, eigh*	Gr. 1 *ay* Gr. 2 *ai* Gr. 4 *ei, eigh*
• Long *e* – *ee* (seed), *ea* (beach), *ie* (chief)	WW	Gr. 1 *ea, ee* Gr. 2 *ie*	Gr. 2 *ee, ea* Gr. 3 *ie*
• Long *i* – *igh* (high), *ie* (pie)	WW	Gr. 1 *igh, ie*	Gr. 2 *igh, ie*
• Long *o* – *oa* (boat), *ow* (snow), *oe* (toe)	WW	Gr. 1 *oa, ow, oe*	Gr. 1 *ow* Gr. 2 *oa, oe*

Phonetic/Morphemic Element	**Spelling Stage**[1]	**Grade Level**	
		Reading	Spelling
• Long *u* – *oo* (moo), *ew* (new), *ui* (suit), *ue* (blue)	WW	Gr. 1 *oo, ew, ue* Gr. 2 *ui*	Gr. 2 *oo, ew, ue* Gr. 3 *ui*
• /oi/ (coin), /oy/ (boy)	WW	Gr. 1	Gr. 2
• /ow/ (cow), /ou/ (out)	WW	Gr. 1	Gr. 2
• /aw/ (paw), /au/ (pause)	WW	Gr. 1	Gr. 2
• /oo/ (book)	WW	Gr. 1	Gr. 2
R-Controlled Syllables (*ar, er/ir/ur, or*)	WW	Gr. 1	Gr. 1 *ar, or* Gr. 3 *er/ir/ur*
More complex R-controlled vowels -*air*, -*are*, -*ear*, -*eer*, -*ire*, -*oar*, -*ore*, -*ure*	WW	Gr. 2	Gr. 3
Regularly spelled one-syllable words	LN/WW	Gr. 1 (in context and out of context)	Gr. 1 (closed syllable words) Gr. 2 and above
Contractions e.g. I'm, he's, could've, doesn't	WW	Gr 1 (simple) Gr. 2 (advanced)	Gr. 2 (simple) Gr. 3 (advanced)
Consonant –*le* Syllables (C-le) e.g. candle, table, gurgle		Gr. 2	Gr. 4
Silent Letters *kn* (knife), *gn* (gnat), *wr* (wrap), *mb* (comb), *gh* (ghost)	WW	Gr. 2	

Phonetic/Morphemic Element	Spelling Stage[1]	Grade Level	
		Reading	**Spelling**
Complex consonant phonograms -*tch* (ditch), -*dge* (fudge), -*ge* (page), -*ck* (lock)	WW	Gr. 1	Gr. 2
Regularly spelled two-syllable words	SJ	Gr. 1 (both syllables are closed) Gr. 2 (any of the six regular syllable patterns)	Gr. 3-4 and above
Trigraphs (*shr-, thr-, squ-, spl-, str-, scr-, spr-*)	WW	Gr. 2	Gr. 2
Possessives (show ownership or relationship)		Gr. 2	Gr. 4 and above
Homophones (words that share the same pronunciation but differ in their meaning and spelling) e.g. plane/plain, to/two/too	WW/SJ		Gr. 3 and above
Homographs (words that are spelled alike but have different pronunciations and meanings related to stress placement) e.g. **con**tract/con**tract**, **re**fuse/re**fuse**	SJ	Gr. 3 and above	N/A
Words with **inflectional endings (no base change)** -*s* (cats), -*es* (boxes), -*ing* (jumping), -*ed* (helped, yelled, landed)	WW/SJ	Gr. 1/Gr. 2	Gr. 2 –*s*, -*ing*, -*ed* Gr. 3 –*es* (when words end in *ch, sh, ss, s,* and *x*)
Understands that some word endings (suffixes) add a certain meaning to the word and their spelling does not change despite having distinct pronunciations e.g. –*ed* pronounced as /id/ in *landed*, /t/ in *helped*, /d/ in *yelled*; plural –*s* pronounced as /z/ in *dogs*	WW	Gr. 1	

Phonetic/Morphemic Element	Spelling Stage[1]	Grade Level	
		Reading	**Spelling**
Soft & Hard *c* and *g*	WW/SJ	Gr. 2	Gr. 3 (one-syll. words) Gr. 4 and above (multisyll. words)
Spelling of final /k/ sound (-*ck*, -*ke*, -*k*, -*ic*) in multisyllabic words	SJ	Gr. 1 (except –*ic* – Gr. 3)	Gr. 3

Forms and uses **irregular plurals** (i.e. words may change pronunciation and spelling in the plural form) e.g. wife/wives, goose/geese	SJ		Gr. 3 and above
Forms and uses **irregular past tense verbs** (i.e. words may change pronunciation and spelling in the plural form) e.g. speak/spoke, throw/threw			Gr. 3 and above
Across-Syllable Patterns **(add suffix with base word change)** Rules that involve a change to the spelling of a <u>one-syllable</u> base word when adding a suffix. A letter may be:			
• Dropped (e.g. like + ed = liked) i.e. adding to base words ending with *e*	SJ	Gr. 2	Gr. 4
• Doubled (e.g. hop + ing = hopping) i.e. adding to base words with a short vowel	SJ	Gr. 2	Gr. 4
• Changed (e.g. fly + es = flies) i.e. adding to base words ending in *y*	SJ	Gr. 2	Gr. 4

Phonetic/Morphemic Element	**Spelling Stage**[1]	**Grade Level**	
		Reading	Spelling
Across-Syllable Patterns (*within* word) Doubling principle applied to syllable junctures *within* words (i.e. doublet at juncture to mark short vowels) e.g. blizzard, pillow, forbidden, permitted)	SJ	Gr. 2	Gr. 3 and above
Different spellings for /sh/ sound: *ti* says /sh/ in word endings (*-tion, -tial, -tient, -tious, -tian*); *ci* says /sh/ in word endings (*-cial, -cient, -cious, -cian*); *ch* says /sh/ in words of French origin (e.g. chef)		Gr. 3 (/sh/ = *ti* in *-tion, -tious, -tial si* in *-sion; ci* in *-cious, -cial*) Gr.4 and above (all others)	Gr. 3 and above
Age-appropriate words of Greek origin with the following letter configurations: *y* = short *i* (symbol); *ph* = /f/ (phobia); *ch* = /k/ (chemistry)	DC	Gr. 4 and above	Gr. 5 and above
Across-Syllable Patterns **(add suffix with base word change)** Rules that involve a change to the spelling of a <u>multisyllabic</u> base word when adding a suffix. A letter may be:			

Phonemic Awareness and Phonics: Knowledge to Practice

• Dropped (e.g. excite + ed = excited, fame + ous = famous)	DC	Gr. 3	Gr. 5 and above
• Doubled (e.g. permit + ed = permitted, forgot + en = forgotten)	DC	Gr. 3	Gr. 5 and above
• Changed (e.g. reply + ed = replied, baby + es = babies)	DC	Gr. 3	Gr. 5 and above

Phonetic/Morphemic Element	Spelling Stage[1]	Grade Level	
		Reading	Spelling
Identifies related words (e.g. addition, additional) based on known root		Introduce in Gr. 2 ongoing. Note: the process of acquiring the ability to see connections among related words is developmental	
Accent/Syllable Stress	WW/SJ	Introduce in Gr. 2 ongoing	
Schwa Sound	SJ	Introduce in Gr. 3 ongoing	
Final unaccented syllable e.g. tab<u>le</u>/tot<u>al</u>/ang<u>el</u>; cap<u>tain</u>/hu<u>man</u>/woo<u>den</u>/mel<u>on</u>; bar<u>ber</u>/act<u>or</u>	SJ/DC	Introduce in Gr. 4 ongoing	
Spells vowel team patterns, silent *e* pattern, r-controlled vowels correctly in the stressed syllable of a multisyllabic word	SJ	Introduce in Gr. 4 ongoing	
Grade-Appropriate **High Frequency Words**		Explicitly taught in K-1 only; Grs. 2 and beyond these words are learned as "rule breakers" during word study	
Prefixes (Basic)	SJ/DC	Introduce in Gr. 1 - ongoing See attached list	
Suffixes	SJ/DC		
Latin Roots	DC	Introduce in Gr. 4 – ongoing See attached list	
Greek Combining Forms	DC		

Phonetic/Morphemic Element	Spelling Stage[1]	Grade Level	
		Reading	Spelling
Prefixes (Assimilated)	DC		

(Prefixes that change spelling, depending on the first letter of the root or base word, for ease of pronunciation) e.g. *in*- changes its spelling to <u>ir</u>regular, <u>il</u>logical, <u>im</u>possible		Introduce in Gr. 5 but this concept is typically addressed in middle school	
Phonetically regular, multisyllabic words composed of multiple affixes and/or roots e.g. preventative, unremarkable, telescopic		Gr. 3 and above (in context and out of context)	Gr. 5 and above

[1]There is widespread acceptance by researchers that children progress through spelling stages. In general, stage theories divide spelling development into five periods or phases; however, the labels for these stages vary. This chart uses the following labels: LN (Letter Name), WW (Within Word Pattern), SJ (Syllable Juncture), and DC (Derivational Constancy) from *Word Journeys* by Kathy Ganske. Only four stages are included because the first, or Emergent, stage of spelling development is a preliterate phase.

[2]This list includes the most common spellings, but does not include all possible spellings, for a given vowel sound. The following vowel teams are not explicitly introduced; instead, they should be taught on a need-to-know basis as students encounter them in reading or writing:

Long *a* – *ea* (steak)   Long *u* – *ue* (blue), *ou* (soup),   Pronunciations of *ough*
                                  eu (feud)
Long *e* – *ey* (key)   Short *e* – *ea* (head)

⁺ Syllable division rules - VC/CV (nap/kin), V/CV (pi/lot), VC/V (lem/on), V/V (li/on), VC/CCV (hun/dred)

Phonemic Awareness and Phonics: Knowledge to Practice

Sample lesson design for the phonemic awareness domain

Component	Purpose	Example
Objectives • Content objective(s)	Connects content knowledge to the core standards	CCSS. ELA RF K.2.B Count, pronounce, blend, and segment syllables in spoken words.
• Learning objective(s)	States the key learning(s) and goal(s) of the lesson	Student will segment words into syllables.
• Language objective(s)	Specifies the language that students need to learn and use to meet the lesson's content and learning objectives – essential for English Learners (ELs)	Student demonstrates understanding of syllable segmentation. Syllable segmentation is an important phonological awareness skill that requires breaking a spoken word into its syllable components. Skill in breaking words into syllables reflects a growing awareness of the vowel sounds in words, since every syllable must have a vowel sound. Syllable awareness is important for both reading and spelling words.
Background Knowledge (Includes both content knowledge and knowledge of students' assessment performance)	• Identifies prerequisite knowledge for the lesson that includes what the student has learned or must know about the topic to successfully master the objectives. • Utilizes formative assessment data to identify instructional goals	Review that our mouths open and chins drop each time we say a vowel sound. This awareness can help us determine how many syllables are in a word.[1]
Introduction of new skill, idea, or content	Provides an explicit explanation (including model/demonstration) to introduce the new skill, idea, or concept	We have been learning to listen for the number of syllables in words. We can tell how many syllables are in a word by the number of times our chins drop while we say the word. Today we are going to practice identifying how many syllables are in words from the story *Goldilocks and the Three Bears* (e.g., **bear** (1), **porridge** (2), and **Goldilocks** (3)). When we decide how many syllables are in the word, we will put that word in our "Going on a Trip" suitcases based on the number of syllables. When all the words are in a suitcase, we will check to

Component	Purpose	Example
		be sure we have packed them with words with the same number of syllables.
Instructional Activity for Guided Practice	Describes the required materials and step-by-step procedures for guiding students through an activity to support their understanding and to provide opportunities to practice the new skill or concept. Activities may also include the following elements: • Check for Understanding and Reteach (if necessary) • Independent Practice	See the **Going on a Trip** activity in the Activities for Instruction and Informal Assessment page 26.
Formative Assessment(s)	Specifies student performance tasks and data to demonstrate mastery of objective(s)	Students will accurately identify the number of syllables in a spoken word.
Review and close	Provides a recap of the new learning, connecting the content, learning and language objective.	"Today we learned how to listen to words from a story to identify the number of syllable the word has. This helps us learn to say new words."

[1]Phonemic awareness activities are essential to facilitate learning to pronounce new vocabulary. For this reason, syllable segmentation activities should be incorporated into the introduction of vocabulary when reading to students. Vocabulary representing a varying number of syllables can be selected from both narrative and informational text for use with this activity.

The Alphabet Chant

A B C D E F G 👏

H I J K L M N 👏

O P Q 👏

R S T 👏

U V W 👏

X Y Z 👏

Now I never will forget, how to say the alphabet.

Sarah Wager, Noah Webster School, 2007

The Alphabet Chant

a b c d e f g 👏

h i j k l m n 👏

o p q 👏

r s t 👏

u v w 👏

x y z 👏

Now I never will forget, how to say the alphabet.

Sarah Wager, Noah Webster School, 2007

The Vowel Song
(Sung to the tune Are You Sleeping?)

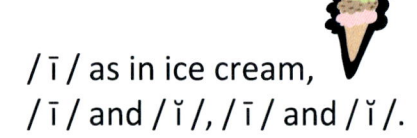

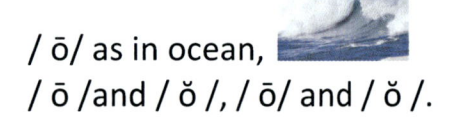

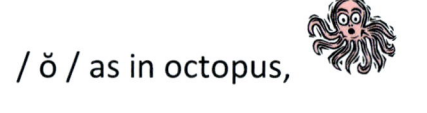

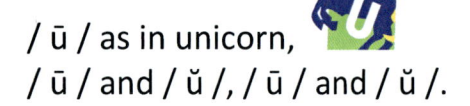

A makes two sounds, a makes two sounds, / ā /and / ă /, / ā / and / ă /.

/ ā / as in acorn,　　　　　　　　/ ă / as in apple,
/ ā / and / ă /, / ā / and / ă /.

E makes two sounds, e makes two sounds, / ē / and / ĕ /, / ē /and / ĕ /.

/ ē / as in eagle,　　　　　　　　/ ĕ / as in echo,
/ ē / and / ĕ /, / ē / and / ĕ /.

I makes two sounds, i makes two sounds, / ī /and / ĭ /, / ī /and/ ĭ /

/ ī / as in ice cream,　　　　　　/ ĭ / as in itch,
/ ī / and / ĭ /, / ī / and / ĭ /.

O makes two sounds, o makes two sounds, / ō / and / ŏ /, / ō /and / ŏ /.

/ ō/ as in ocean,　　　　　　　　/ ŏ / as in octopus,
/ ō /and / ŏ /, / ō/ and / ŏ /.

U makes two sounds, u makes two sounds, / ū /and / ŭ /, / ū /and / ŭ /.

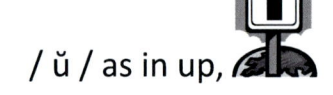

/ ū / as in unicorn, 　　　　　　　/ ŭ / as in up,
/ ū / and / ŭ /, / ū / and / ŭ /.

Cue words for the letters of the alphabet

The following pictures are suggested as cues for the beginning sounds for the letters of the alphabet, with the exception of the letter **x**, which illustrates the final sound as in **box**. Other pictures can be substituted being careful to avoid selecting objects where the initial sound is the first sound in a consonant blend or a digraph.

A	apple
B	bear
C	car
D	dog
E	echo
F	fish
G	goat
H	house

Phonemic Awareness and Phonics: Knowledge to Practice

I	itch
J	jar
K	kite
L	lion
M	moon
N	nurse
O	octopus
P	pig
Q	queen
R	rose

S	sock
T	turtle
U	up
V	Valentine
W	walrus
X	box
Y	yellow
Z	zebra

Phonemic Awareness and Phonics: Knowledge to Practice

Stroke Descriptions for Continuous Manuscript Letters

a – Around, down.

b – Down, up, around.

c – Around, stop.

d – Around, up, down.

e – Across, around, stop.

f – Curve, down. Cross.

g – Around, down, hook.

h – Down, hump.

i – Down, dot.

j – Down. hook, dot.

k – Down. Slant in, slant out.

l – Down.

m – Down, hump, hump.

n – Down, hump.

o – Top, around, close.

p – Down, up, around.

q – Around, down, hook.

r – Down, up, over.

s – Curve, slant, curve.

t – Down. Cross.

u – Down, curve up, down.

v – Slant down, slant up.

w – Slant down, slant up, slant down, slant up.

x – Slant right. Slant left.

y – Slant right. Slant left.

z – Across, slant down left, across.

Retrieved from http://www.neuhaus.org

Phoneme-Grapheme Map

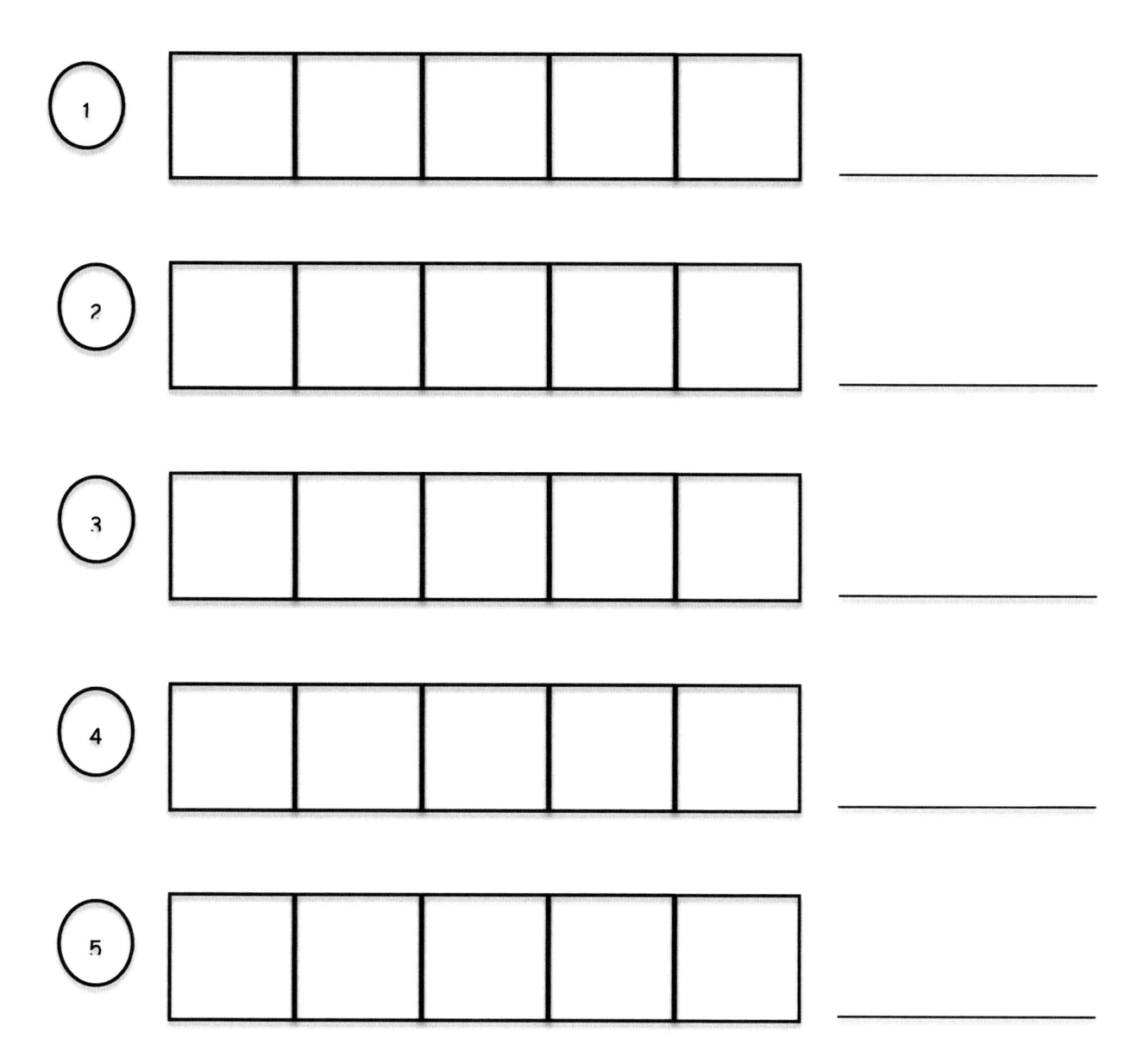

① ☐☐☐☐☐ _____

② ☐☐☐☐☐ _____

③ ☐☐☐☐☐ _____

④ ☐☐☐☐☐ _____

⑤ ☐☐☐☐☐ _____

Phonetically Irregular Words[1]

again	have	the
answer	kind	their
any	know	there
are	learn	they
because	listen	though
been	live	through
both	many	to
brought	most	two
cold	mother	want
color	move	was
come	of	water
could	off	were
do	often	where
does	old	who
earth	once	what
enough	one	whose
eyes	only	word
father	other	work
find	people	would
friend	put	you
from	said	your
give	should	
great	some	

[1] The part of the word in red deviates from the predictable sound-symbol correspondences.

First 100 High Frequency Words

1. the	26. or	51. out	76. its
2. of	27. by	52. them	77. who
3. and	28. one	53. then	78. now
4. a	29. had	54. she	79. people
5. to	30. not	55. many	80. my
6. in	31. but	56. some	81. made
7. is	32. what	57. so	82. over
8. you	33. all	58. these	83. did
9. that	34. were	59. would	84. down
10. it	35. when	60. other	85. only
11. he	36. we	61. into	86. way
12. for	37. there	62. has	87. find
13. was	38. can	63. more	88. use
14. on	39. an	64. her	89. may
15. are	40. your	65. two	90. water
16. as	41. which	66. like	91. long
17. with	42. their	67. him	92. little
18. his	43. said	68. see	93. very
19. they	44. if	69. time	94. after
20. at	45. do	70. could	95. words
21. be	46. will	71. no	96. called
22. this	47. each	72. make	97. just
23. from	48. about	73. than	98. where
24. I	49. how	74. first	99. most
25. have	50. up	75. been	100. know

Fluency Word Table

										Number of words
										10
										20
										30
										40
										50
										60
										70
										80
										90
										100

1st Trial _____   2nd Trial _____

Fluency Graph

Number of Correct Words Per Minute								
170								
160								
150								
140								
130								
120								
110								
100								
90								
80								
70								
60								
50								
40								
35								
20								
10								
Title								
Date								

Phonemic Awareness and Phonics: Knowledge to Practice

Hasbrouck & Tindal (2017)

From Hasbrouck, J. & Tindal, G. (2017). An update to compiled ORF norms (Technical Report No. 1702). Eugene, OR. Behavioral Research and Teaching, University of Oregon.

Grade	%ile	Fall WCPM*	Winter WCPM*	Spring WCPM*
1	90		97	116
1	75		59	91
1	50		29	60
1	25		16	34
1	10		9	18
2	90	111	131	148
2	75	84	109	124
2	50	50	84	100
2	25	36	59	72
2	10	23	35	43
3	90	134	161	166
3	75	104	137	139
3	50	83	97	112
3	25	59	79	91
3	10	40	62	63
4	90	153	168	184
4	75	125	143	160
4	50	94	120	133
4	25	75	95	105
4	10	60	71	83
5	90	179	183	195
5	75	153	160	169
5	50	121	133	146
5	25	87	109	119
5	10	64	84	102
6	90	185	195	204
6	75	159	166	173
6	50	132	145	146
6	25	112	116	122
6	10	89	91	91

*WCPM = words correct per minute

Syllable Inspector Rule Card - Closed

	Closed: **VC** **CCVC** **CVCC** **CVC** **CCVCC**
👁	1. One (1) vowel, followed by
👁	2. One (1) or more consonants
👂	3. The *short* sound for the vowel

Phonemic Awareness and Phonics: Knowledge to Practice

Syllable Inspector Rule Card - Open

	Open: **C**V V
👁	1. One (1) vowel at the end
👁	2. NO consonants after the vowel
🔊	3. The long sound for the vowel

Syllable Inspector Rule Card – Silent e

	Silent e **VCe**
👁	1. One (1) vowel, followed by
👁	2. One (1) consonant and a final "e"
👂	3. The *long* sound for the vowel

Syllable Inspector Rule Card – Vowel Team (Talkers)

	Vowel Team VV (Talkers)
👁	1. Two (2) vowels side-by-side
	2. First one does the talking and says its name
👂	The long sound for the vowel

Syllable Inspector Rule Card – Vowel Team (Whiners)

	Vowel Team VV (Whiners)
👁	1. Two (2) vowels side-by-side
	2. Make whining sounds, like when you fall down and say "ow," "aw," and "oi."
👂	The different – whiney—sound for the vowel

Syllable Inspector Rule Card – r-controlled

	r-controlled Vr
👁	1. One (1) vowel followed by **r**
	2. The **r** is **bossy** and takes over the sound of the vowel. The vowel can't say its short or long sound, but says a sound with the **r**.
👂	ar / or
	er, ir, ur

154

Syllable Inspector Rule Card – Consonant-le

	Consonant-le (C – le)
👁	1. A consonant – le at the end of a two-syllable word
👂	You hear a vowel sound between the consonant and the le, but you don't see it. It doesn't sound like a short or a long vowel sound, because the l bosses it and makes the e silent.

Syllable Inspector Rule Card - Schwa Card

	Schwa
👁	4. One of the vowels: **a, e, i, o, u**
👂	5. The short sound for u ⬆ and short i

Sample lesson design for the phonics domain

Component	Purpose	Example
Objectives • Content objective(s)	Connects content knowledge to the core standards	CCSS. ELA RF 1.3.A Know the spelling-sound correspondences for common consonant digraphs.
• Learning objective(s)	States the key learning(s) and goal(s) of the lesson	Student will read and spell words with consonant digraphs in the initial position (e.g., **ch-** as in **chip**, **sh-** as in **ship**, **th-** as in **thin** and **wh-** as in **whip**).
• Language objective(s)	Specifies the language that students need to learn and use to meet the lesson's content and learning objectives – essential for English Learners (ELs)	Student demonstrates understanding of the concept and word digraph. Usually we use one letter to represent one sound in English. Some sounds are represented by two letters. For example, the single sound / ch /, as in **chip**, is represented by the letters **c + h**. The word has three sounds (/ ch / / ĭ / / p /) but is written with four letters (**chip**).
Background Knowledge (Includes both content knowledge and knowledge of students' assessment performance)	• Identifies prerequisite knowledge for the lesson that includes what the student has learned or must know about the topic to successfully master the objectives. • Utilizes formative assessment data to identify instructional goals	Use the **Say It and Move It** activity[1] to engage students in listening for familiar and new phonemes for the lesson. Use words like **chip**, **chain**, and **much**. [1,2] Next, review blending (decoding) and segmenting (spelling) several CVC words that begin with the / h /, / s /, and / ĭ / sounds (e.g., **hip**, **sip**, and **tin**).
Introduction of new skill, idea, or content	Provides an explicit explanation (including model/demonstration) to introduce the new skill, idea, or concept	"We have been reading and spelling words in which each sound is represented by a single letter. Today we are going to learn to read and spell words that have sounds represented by two letters. These special sounds are called digraph (i.e., di = 2; graph = letters). When we hear the digraph sounds, we use two letters to represent the sound. We will use our sound-letter maps and our tokens. Then we will practice spelling and reading those words."

Component	Purpose	Example
Instructional Activity for Guided Practice	Describes the required materials and step-by-step procedures for guiding students through an activity to support their understanding and to provide opportunities to practice the new skill or concept. Activities may also include the following elements: • Check for Understanding and Reteach (if necessary) • Independent Practice	See the **Sound - Letter Maps** activity in the Activities for Instruction and Informal Assessment page 34.
Formative Assessment(s)	Specifies student performance tasks and data to demonstrate mastery of objective(s)	Students will accurately and independently read and spell words consonant digraphs in the initial position.
Review and close	Provides a recap of the new learning, connecting the content, learning and language objective.	"Today we learned how to read and spell words with a consonant digraph at the beginning of the word. We call these sounds digraphs because one sound is represented by two (di) letters (graphs)."

[1] The **Say It and Move It** activity is available on page 28.

[2] Within every phonics lesson, there is a phonemic awareness component to activate attention to phonemes prior to mapping to letters.

Words and Phrases for *Cal and Tramp Camp*

ran	ran up
him	to him
set	set up camp
in	in back
Cal	of Cal's house
back	go back
on	on Cal's lap
got	got in the tent
Dan	Dan and Tramp
his	his dog Tramp

References and Resources

Phonemic Awareness

Adams, M. (1990) *Beginning to read: Thinking and learning about print.* Cambridge, MA: MIT Press

Adams, M.J., Foorman, B.R., Lundberg, I. & Beeler,T. (1998). The elusive phoneme. *American Educator Spring/Summer* 18-29.

Ball, E.W. & Blachman, B.A. (1991). Does phoneme awareness training in kindergarten make a difference in early word recognition and developmental spelling? *Reading Research Quarterly 26*, 49–66.

Blachman B. (1989). Phonological awareness and word recognition: Assessment and intervention. In Kamhi G., Carts W. (Eds.), *Reading disabilities: A Developmental language perspective,* 133–158, Boston: College-Hill Press.

Blachman, B. A., Ball, E. W., Black, R., & Tangel, D. M. (2000). *Road to the Code: A Phonological Awareness Program for Young Children.* Brookes Publishing: Baltimore, MD

Bowey, J. (2000). Recent developments in language acquisition and reading research: The phonological basis of children's reading difficulties. *Australian Educational and Developmental Psychologist 17*(1), 5-31.

Byrne, B., Fielding-Barnsley, R. & Ashley, L. (2000). Effects of preschool phoneme identity training after six years: Outcome level distinguished from rate of response. *Journal of Educational Psychology 92*, 659–667.

Ehri, L. (2004). Teaching phonemic awareness and phonics: An explanation of the national reading panel meta-analysis. In P. McCardle and V. Chhabra (Eds) *The voice of evidence in reading research*, 153-187, Baltimore, MD: Brookes Publishing.

Chall, J. (1983). *Stages of reading development,* 10-24. New York: McGraw-Hill.

Fowler, A.E., (1991). How early phonological development might set the stage for phoneme awareness. In S.A. Brady & D.P. Shankweiler (Eds). *Phonological processes in literacy: A tribute to Isabelle Y. Liberman.* Hillsdale, NJ: Lawrence Erlbaum Associates.

Kilpatrick, D. A. (2015). *Essentials of assessing, preventing, and overcoming reading difficulties.* N.J.: John Wiley & Sons.

Liberman, Y., Shankweiler D., & Liberman, A.M. (1989). The alphabetic principle and learning to read. In D. Shankweiler and I.Y. Liberman (Eds.), *Phonology and reading disability: Solving the reading puzzle*, 1-3. Ann Arbor: University of Michigan Press.

Marshall, J. (1998). *Goldilocks and the three bears.* New York: Picture Puffin Books.

Mesmer, H.A. (2001) Decodable text: A review of what we know. *Reading Research and Instruction, Winter 40* (2), 121 – 142.

Moats, L. (1999). Teaching reading is rocket science: what expert teachers of reading should know and be able to do. *American Educator.* AFT: Washington D.C.

Moats, L., & Tolman, C. (2009). The development of phonological skills. Retrieved October 16, 2014, from http://www.readingrockets.org/article/development-phonological-skills

National Reading Panel (US), National Institute of Child Health, & Human Development (US). (2000). *Report of the national reading panel: Teaching children to read: An evidence-based assessment of the scientific research literature on reading and its implications for reading instruction: Reports of the subgroups.* National Institute of Child Health and Human Development, National Institutes of Health.

Shankweiler, D. (1989). How problems of comprehension are related to difficulties in decoding. In D. Shankweiler & I.Y. Liberman (Eds.), *Phonology and reading disability: Solving the reading puzzle*, 35–68. Ann Arbor: University of Michigan Press.

Shankweiler D. & Fowler, A.E. (2004). Questions people ask about the role of phonological processes in learning to read. *Reading and Writing: An Interdisciplinary Journal 17*, 483-515.

Spear-Swerling, L., & Brucker, P. (2004). Preparing novice teachers to develop basic reading and spelling skills in children. *Annals of Dyslexia* 54, 332-364.

Torgesen, J. (2002). The prevention of reading difficulties. *Journal of School Psychology* 40(1), 7-26.

Yopp, H.K., & Yopp, R.H. (2000). Supporting phonemic awareness development in the classroom. *The Reading Teacher 54(2)*, 130-143.

Phonics

Adams, M. J. (1990). *Beginning to read: Thinking and learning about print.* Cambridge: The MIT Press.

Adams, M. J. (1997). The great debate: Then and now. *Annals of Dyslexia 47(1)*, 265-276.

Cabell, S. Q., Tortorelli, L. S., & Gerde, H. K. (2013). How do I write...? Scaffolding preschoolers' early writing skills. *The Reading Teacher 66(8)*, 650-659.

Carreker, S. (2005). Spelling instruction: Foundation of reading and ornament of writing. *Perspectives on Language and Literacy 31(3)*, 22–25.

Chall, J.S. (1967). *Learning to read: The great debate.* New York: McGraw-Hill.

Cheatham, J. P., & Allor, J. H. (2012). The influence of decodability in early reading text on reading achievement: A review of the evidence. *Reading and Writing 25(9)*, 2223-2246.

Cheyney, W.S. and Cohen, E.J. (1999). *Focus on phonics: Assessment and instruction.* Bothell, WA: The Wright Group/McGraw-Hill, pp. 32 – 33.

Ehri, L. C. (2014). Orthographic mapping in the acquisition of sight word reading, spelling memory, and vocabulary learning. *Scientific Studies of Reading 18(1)*, 5-21.

Ehri, L. (2005). Learning to read words: theory, findings, and issues. *Scientific Studies of Reading 9(2)*, 167-188.

Ehri, L. C. (2000). Learning to read and learning to spell: Two sides of a coin. *Topics in Language Disorders 20(3)*, 19-36.

Ehri, L., & McCormick, S. (1998). Phases of word learning: implications for instruction with delayed and disabled readers. *Reading & Writing Quarterly 14(2)*, 135-164.

Ehri, L. C. (1997). Learning to read and learning to spell are one and the same, almost. In C. Perfetti, L. Rieben, & M. Fayol (Eds.), *Learning to spell: Research, theory, and practice across languages.* Mahwah, NJ: Erlbaum.

Ehri, L. C. (1986). Sources of difficulty in learning to spell and read. *Advances in Developmental & Behavioral Pediatrics 7,* 121-195.

Hanna, P. R., Hanna, J. S., Bergquist, S. R., Hodges, R. E., & Rudorf, E. H. (1966). Needed research in spelling. *Elementary English 43(1)*, 60-89.

Hanna, P.R., Hodges, R.E., & Hanna, J.S. (1971). *Spelling: Structure and strategies.* Boston: Houghton Mifflin Company.

Irujo, S. (2007). What does research tell us about teaching reading to English language learners. *ELL Outlook.*

Joshi, R. M., Treiman, R., Carreker, S., & Moats, L. C. (2008). How words cast their spell. *American Educator 32(4)*, 6-16.

Kilpatrick, D.A., (2015). *Essentials of assessing, preventing, and overcoming reading difficulties.* New Jersey: Wiley.

Martin, B., & Carle, E. (1984). *Brown bear, brown bear.* New York: Puffin books.

Mesmer, H. A. E. (2005). Text decodability and the first-grade reader. *Reading & Writing Quarterly 21(1),* 61-86.

Neuhaus, G.F. (2003). What does It take to read a letter? *Perspectives on Language and Literacy*, Winter, 27 – 31.

Piasta, S. & Wagner, R. (2010). Learning letter names and sounds: Effects of instruction, letter type, and phonological process skill. *Journal of Experimental Child Psychology 105*, 324-344.

Rayner, K., Foorman, B. R., Perfetti, C. A., Pesetsky, D., & Seidenberg, M. S. (2001). How psychological science informs the teaching of reading. *Psychological science in the public interest*, 2(2), 31-74.

Seidenberg, M. (2017). *Language at the speed of sight.* New York: Basic Books.

Share, D. L. (1995). Phonological recoding and self-teaching: Sine qua non of reading acquisition. *Cognition 55(2)*, 151-218.

Spear-Swerling, L. (2015). A Bridge Too Far?: Implications of the Common Core for Students with Different Kinds of Reading Problems. *Perspectives on Language and Literacy*, 41(2), 25.

Spear-Swerling, L. (2018). Structured literacy and typical literacy practices: Understanding differences to create instructional opportunities. Teaching Exceptional Children.

Snow, C., Burns, S., & Griffin, P. (Eds.). (1998). *Preventing reading difficulties in young children.* Washington, DC: National Academy Press (NAP).

Thomson, S. L. (2009). *Where do polar bears live?* New York: Harper Collins.

Weiser, B. L. (2013). Ameliorating reading disabilities early: Examining an effective encoding and decoding prevention instruction model. *Learning Disability Quarterly 36(3),* 161-177.

www.cde.state.co.us/coloradoliteracy/theimportanceofteahchingletternames

Made in the USA
Middletown, DE
05 November 2022